Michaelangelos.

from Liz   FEB 78.

FAMOUS REGIMENTS

The 10th Royal Hussars

FAMOUS REGIMENTS

Edited by
Lt.-General Sir Brian Horrocks

The 10th
Royal Hussars

(Prince of Wales's Own)

by
Michael Brander

Leo Cooper Ltd, London

PRINTED AND BOUND IN ENGLAND BY
HAZELL WATSON AND VINEY LTD
AYLESBURY, BUCKS

TO

THE ROYAL HUSSARS
THE PRINCE OF WALES'S OWN

ALSO

OLD COMRADES OF THE TENTH

AND

THE CAVALRY SPIRIT

INTRODUCTION TO THE SERIES
by Lt.-General Sir Brian Horrocks

It is always sad when old friends depart. In the last few years many famous old regiments have disappeared, merged into larger formations.

I suppose this process is inevitable; strategy and tactics are always changing, forcing the structure of the Army to change too. But the memories of the past still linger in minds now trained to great technical proficiency and surrounded by sophisticated equipment. Nevertheless the disappearance of these well-known names as separate units marks the end of a military epoch; but we must never forget that, throughout the years, each of these regiments has carved for itself a special niche in British history. The qualities of the British character, both good and bad, which helped England to her important position in the world can be seen at work in the regiments of the old Army. To see why these regiments succeeded under Marlborough and Wellington yet failed in the American War of Independence should help us in assessing the past.

Though many Battle Honours were won during historic campaigns, the greatest contribution which our regiments have made to the British Empire is rarely mentioned: this has surely been the protection they have afforded to those indomitable British merchants who in search of fresh markets spread our influence all over the world. For some of these this involved spending many years in stinking garrisons overseas where their casualties from disease were often far greater than those suffered on active service.

The main strength of our military system has always

lain in the fact that regimental roots were planted deep into the British countryside in the shape of the Territorial Army whose battalions are also subject to the cold winds of change. This ensured the closest possible link between civilian and military worlds, and built up a unique county and family *esprit de corps* which exists in no other army in the world. A Cockney regiment, a West Country regiment and a Highland regiment differed from each other greatly, though they fought side by side in scores of battles. In spite of miserable conditions and savage discipline, a man often felt he belonged within the regiment—he shared the background and the hopes of his fellows. That was a great comfort for a soldier. Many times, at Old Comrades' gatherings, some old soldier has come up to me and said, referring to one of the World Wars, 'They were good times, Sir, weren't they?'

They were not good times at all. They were horrible times; but what these men remember and now miss was the comradeship and *esprit de corps* of the old regular regiments. These regiments, which bound men together and helped them through the pain and fear of war, deserve to be recalled.

Regimental histories are usually terribly dull, as the authors are forced to record the smallest operation and include as many names as possible. In this series we have something new. Freed from the tyranny of minute detail, the authors have sought to capture that subtle quarry, the regimental spirit. The history of each regiment is a story of a type of British life now fading away. These stories illuminate the past, and should help us to think more clearly about the military future.

The 10th Royal Hussars

A SPECIAL INTRODUCTION

by Lt.-General Sir Brian Horrocks

I HAVE always had a secret feeling of envy for the British Cavalry. The 10th Hussars are a case in point. My first contact with the regiment came in Aldershot between 1924–27; they had the reputation then of being, with the exception of the Household Cavalry, the most aristocratic and expensive regiment in the British Army. If my memory serves me right H.R.H. The Duke of Gloucester was serving with them at that time as a captain. They were called the 'Shiny Tenth' because their turn-out was reputed to be the smartest of any cavalry regiment in the army.

They also had an impressive list of battle honours to their credit, won in all the major wars in which this country has been engaged.

When I knew them Colonel Malise-Graham and his famous horse Broncho were household names in the show-jumping world.

But mechanisation was rearing its ugly head and we wondered how this regiment so deeply wedded to their horses would take to this new form of warfare.

We need not have worried however. The cavalry regiments took to tanks as ducks to water. They were used to belonging to a Corps d'Elite; stable management had always required grinding hard work, a meticulous attention to detail and dedicated care of their animals. This was now transferred to their tanks and the officers led the way. It became a matter of family, or regimental pride to master this new arm. Although all regiments have their own *esprit de corps*, a good cavalry regiment like the 10th was almost a family affair. Many of the officers and men were the third and fourth generation to have served in this particular regiment and they had grown up with no other thought than to serve in the 10th. A high proportion of the officers were the sons of landowners and had been brought up from childhood with a sense of personal responsibility for the tenants on their estates; this was now transferred to the men under their command.

I realised all this very quickly when they came under my command in the western desert, where the tank was the queen of the battlefield. Their gallantry was unsurpassed; faced by highly trained German forces equipped with weapons that outranged theirs by at least 500 yards, it needed 'guts' of the highest order to launch attack after attack over this open country with burnt-out tanks which had been manned by their own comrades all around them. The action of the 10th Hussars in the Saunnu depression under command of Lt.-Colonel Harvey was just one example. After repeated attacks the whole regiment was reduced to a composite squadron of seven tanks only, but their losses had not been in vain; they had succeeded in saving their brigade headquarters and the Brigade of Guards.

My first contact with them in the desert was in August/September 1942 when a composite regiment of the 10th Hussars, 9th Lancers and Bays, serving with the 7th Armoured Division took part in the Battle of Alam Halfa, when Rommel launched his last all-out attack to capture Egypt on my Corps front and failed.

My most memorable experience, however, was during the Battle of Mareth, when the 1st Armoured Division (of which the 10th Hussars formed part in the 2nd Armoured Brigade) was put under my command for a wide encircling movement around the enemy's right flank when the initial direct attack by 30 Corps along the coastal plain had failed. My attack was made in conjunction with the 2nd New

Zealand Division, who were to punch a hole in the enemy defences through which I proposed to pass the Armoured Formations. This was the most exciting, but worrying, night of my life—I was proposing to pass an armoured division through the 21st German Panzer Division and their 164 Infantry Division, during the night, helped only by a rather weak, watery moon. It was an unheard of manoeuvre and if anything went wrong I knew my neck would be on the block. I could just hear the armchair critics in the London Clubs saying: 'Heavens—the man must be mad.' But I was banking on three things.

(1) The high standard of training in the 1st Armoured Division which alone made this preposterous night manoeuvre possible; (2) for the first time in the war we were given by the R.A.F. for the break-in, the most superb low level attacks on the German positions and (3) the Germans, although good troops, are also slow to react to something new, and this doubtful manoeuvre was very new indeed. I started very bravely with the upper part of my body sticking out of the turret of my tank, but as the advance went on I got lower and lower until only the top of my head was visible. There was too much stuff flying about for comfort.

Anyhow it succeeded—elderly 10th Hussars can now tell their grandchildren (who will of course be dreadfully bored) that they took part in a unique attack which had never been tried before and is never likely to be tried again.

Michael Brander finishes his enthralling history by saying that in October 1969 the 10th and 11th Hussars were merged into the Royal Hussars (Prince of Wales's Own). I cannot imagine two better bedfellows, or should I say stable companions.

'Once a Hussar, always a Hussar.'

Acknowledgements

THIS is necessarily a brief outline history based chiefly on Richard Cannon's *Historical Record of the Tenth*, 1843, *Memoirs of the Tenth Hussars*, by R. S. Liddell, 1891, *A Short History of the X.R.H.*, by Colonel J. Vaughan, 1909, *The Tenth Royal Hussars during the 1914–18 War*, by F. H. D. C. Whitmore, *The 6th Cavalry Brigade 1914–18*, by J. B. Bickersteth, also *The 10th Hussars in the 2nd World War*, edited by Colonel A. Kearsey. Various other sources, such as diaries, letters and Regimental Gazettes, have been used or consulted, but the book could not have been completed on schedule without the willing assistance and encouragement of the staff of Home H.Q., X.R.H., Major R. A. Archer Shee, M.C., and Major T. C. Moorhouse, M.C., also, amongst many others, Colonel D. R. B. Kaye, D.S.O., Colonel C. K. Davy, M.C., and Major General Sir David Dawnay, C.B., D.S.O. Mention must also be made of the helpful and understanding co-operation of the publisher Mr. Leo Cooper. To all these I am most grateful and the book owes much to their help. For any mistakes I am to blame. It is to be hoped that this brief factual outline will give pleasure and interest not only to those connected with the regiment, but also to those who have not had that good fortune and are merely curious to know what makes a fine regiment and a great tradition.

Chapter

I

IN 1715, when the Jacobite rebellion following the
accession of George I threatened the internal peace and
security of the nation, the Regiment was raised in
Hertfordshire and the adjacent counties by Brigadier
Humphrey Gore. It was then known as the 10th Regiment
of Dragoons and the uniform was 'scarlet with buff belts,'
the arms 'a sword, carbine and pair of pistols,' the mounts
were soon standardised as 'not above the size of 15 hands,
very nimble kind of horses that can gallop, with short backs,
broad fillets and clean legs.' The establishment consisted of
six troops, each with three officers, three N.C.Os, a drum-
mer, a haut boy (forerunner of the trumpeter), and forty
privates. Particularly notable was the appointment of Henry
Gore, son of the Colonel, Brigadier Gore, as Captain-
Lieutenant, for this was the first of many such father and
son relationships, or close family connections, amongst
all ranks, often continuing for generations, which were to
become an outstanding feature of the regiment.

Due to the early collapse of the 1715 rebellion the regiment was never in action against the Jacobite forces, but was
employed instead in the suppression of local tumults and
the maintenance of law and order. For the next thirty years
the regiment's principal role continued to be one of law and
revenue enforcement throughout the country entailing
frequent moves from one area to another. This entailed
dispersal around the countryside with troops or squadrons
quartered in public houses of country towns and similar
billets, making collective training difficult, but fostering the
squadron spirit.

The most noteworthy incident in this period was the

interception by a squadron of the regiment in 1743 of 150 deserters from Lord Semphill's Highland Regiment. Originally volunteering on the understanding that they would not have to serve overseas they had deserted with their arms, which they had themselves provided, and were returning to their homes in Scotland, due to a rumour that they were to be posted to the West Indies. Intercepted at Oundle by a squadron of the 10th Dragoons and a squadron of the 3rd Dragoons they surrendered without bloodshed. The three ringleaders were court-martialled and shot as an example, but the Highland Regiment went on to the continent to gain fame and glory, subsequently becoming known in the annals of the British Army as The Black Watch.

Compared with private foot soldiers earning 8d. a day the Dragoons were picked men, well paid at 1s. 9d. a day, but only a portion of their pay was received weekly. The rest was held back and paid in arrears, less deductions for all food other than bread, which was a free issue. The Captain controlled the pay for his troop and expected to make a reasonable profit from feeding them.

Living conditions in the army were hard in the extreme, but it was a hard age. Men could receive several hundred lashes on the triangle in the presence of the regiment drawn up on parade for seemingly trivial offences. When barracks were available the rule was one bed and one blanket per two men and there were only two tubs for washing, emptied daily. Four wives were allowed in each troop, accompanying them on active service, cooking, mending and tending the wounded. Children who survived the rigours of such an upbringing usually stayed with the regiment, the boys as drummers, the girls as wives. Hence, willy nilly, the family atmosphere developed with the Captain of each troop as the head and the Colonel as a minor deity.

For officers, too, life tended to be that of a closed community, but it was always possible for them to exchange, or purchase promotion in another regiment, if they saw no future in their own, or wished to avoid foreign service. The dual principle behind the system of purchase was that by this means the government ensured that men of substance became officers who would safeguard their investment by avoiding misconduct and on retirement would be able to sell out for a lump sum, thus saving the need to provide them with a pension.

A cornetcy in 'Gore's Dragoons' cost £520 (by 1780 nearer £1,000) but his pay was little more than 5s. a day and with deductions amounted to about a fifth of this. Thus, as the majority of officers had purchased their commissions and subsequent promotions, their pay amounted to little more than a modest interest on their purchase price. Promotion however could also be achieved on the death of a senior officer, by appointment on formation of a new regiment, or by raising a given number of recruits. Over the rank of Lt.-Colonel promotion was strictly by seniority, resulting sometimes in a considerable number of retired generals, who received only their pay at their regimental rank, but strange as it seems today this system worked for most of the eighteenth and a good part of the nineteenth centuries.

Brigadier Humphrey Gore was succeeded as Colonel of the Regiment in 1723 by Colonel Charles Churchill and on his death in 1745 as a Lieutenant-General the Colonelcy went to Field Marshal Viscount Cobham. Thus it was as 'Cobham's Dragoons' that the regiment marched against the army of the Young Pretender in 1745. It was not however until 1746 that the 10th Dragoons encountered the rebels at Falkirk. According to an eyewitness: 'the attack was begun by our three regiments of dragoons, who broke through the enemy and behaved like bold fellows, and afterwards rallied again.' Unfortunately the attack was repelled and the Royalist forces under General Hawley were forced to retire, but according to the *London Gazette*: 'the enemy did not pursue, which was owing to the gallant behaviour of two squadrons of Cobham's (Tenth) Dragoons.'

Under the command of the Duke of Cumberland they pursued the retreating Highlanders by forced marches, next encountering a force of a thousand foot and sixty hussars (probably French since this is the first mention of Hussars in Britain) at Strathbogie in Aberdeenshire. On this occasion the rebels escaped, but at Culloden shortly afterwards it was a different story. There the 10th Dragoons, after breaking down a wall on the right flank of the rebel army, charged and 'completed the victory.'

Following this action the 10th reverted to their role of law enforcement and very shortly returned again to the south. On the death of Viscount Cobham in 1749 the Colonelcy was conferred on Major-General John Mordaunt and in 1751 there was a major alteration in their uniform, viz:

'Coats—scarlet, double breasted, without lapels, lined with deep yellow: slit sleeves turned up with deep yellow; the button holes worked with white lace; the buttons of white metal, set on three, four and five together; a slash pocket in each skirt; and a white worsted aiguillette on the right shoulder.

'Waistcoats and breeches—deep yellow.

'Hats—bound with silver lace and ornamented with a black cockade and a white metal loop.

'Boots—of jacked leather.

'Cloaks—of scarlet cloth, with a deep yellow collar and lined with deep yellow shaloon; the buttons set on white frogs or loops with a green stripe down the centre.

'Horse Furniture—of deep yellow cloth, the holster-caps and housing having a border of white lace, with a green stripe down the centre; X.D. embroidered on each corner of the housing on a red ground, within a wreath of roses and thistles; the King's cipher with the crown over it, and X.D. underneath, embroidered on the holster caps.'

'Officers—distinguished by silver lace; their coats and waistcoats bound with silver embroidery; the button holes worked with silver; and a crimson sash worn across the left shoulder.'

It is thus easy to picture the dashing appearance of the regiment on the outbreak of war with France in 1755, especially with the addition of a seventh troop, known as the Light Troop and equipped as Light Dragoons, which was then added to the strength. The following year, on the outbreak of the Seven Years War on the continent, Thomas O. Mordaunt reinforcing his family ties was gazetted Captain-Lieutenant. Then in 1757 Major-General Sir John Mordaunt commanded an ill-fated seaborne attack, known as the Rochefort Expedition, in which the 10th Dragoons participated. Ten battalions were embarked from the Isle of Wight under convoy of sixteen sail commanded by Admiral Hawke, but apart from capturing the Isle d'aix and occupying it briefly the expedition achieved nothing, being bedevilled by politics and intrigue. On his return Sir John was court-martialled and honourably acquitted.

Apparently unperturbed by this fiasco another expedition was planned in 1758, in which the Light Troop took part under Brigadier Eliott and the Duke of Marlborough, but apart from destroying shipping, naval stores and magazines in the port of St. Malo this also achieved very little. Later in the year the entire regiment embarked for Germany under the Duke of Marlborough's command. They disembarked at Embden and without being engaged in any important action passed their first winter on the continent in Paderborn.

Some illuminating glimpses of life with the regiment during this campaign may be had from letters written by Major Richard Davenport to his brother at home. Since Lt.-Colonel William Augustus Pitt was away for long periods the effective command devolved on Major Davenport.

> '3rd January, 1759. Lathen. I am sorry I can give Mrs Moss no other account of her husband than that he died at Munster. As to his things, whatever he had is lost. When a man goes into hospital his wallet, with his necessaries are sent with him, but nothing ever returns. They are all plundered by the nurses.'

> '21st May, 1759. 4 leagues from Munster. The dirty village and peasants barn which was my lot in winter is changed to a handsome modern house. We had three Balls a week since we came here, but alas! this very evening as we were drinking tea and singing French songs there came a scoundrel full gallop, blowing a damned squeaking horn and produces an order to march to morrow morning.'

> '1st August, 1759. Minden. We have this day gained a victory. I and all your friends are well.'

(At Minden the British Cavalry was on the right flank and when the French began to run Prince Ferdinand ordered Lord George, Viscount Sackville to charge, but for some reason, possibly misunderstanding the order, he did not do so. He was recalled to England, court-martialled for failure to obey an order and disgraced.)

> 'November 1759. We remained out from 8 o'clock in the evening of the 27th till the next afternoon, but nothing happened. We continue very alert and some squadrons are under arms constantly.'

Major Davenport's last entry ran:

> '12th July, 1760. We get but little sleep and that when we catch it, for some days past oftener on the ground than in our tents, with all this and want of regular meals I was never in better health and spirits.'

At the battle of Warburg on July 31, 1760, the British Cavalry under Lord Granby redeemed their failure at

Minden by charging the French and completely routing them. Many squadrons became detached from their regiments in the charge. The left squadron of the Tenth commanded by Major Davenport encountered an enemy German Grenadier regiment. Mistaking them for their Hessian allies Major Davenport halted the squadron within seventy yards of their line. They opened fire, killing him and another officer instantly and the horses of two others. Captain Mordaunt, the only mounted officer left, at once took command and in spite of another volley led a charge which overthrew the entire Grenadier regiment. The squadron captured 300 of the Grenadiers, including their Colonel, who surrendered to Captain Mordaunt. The spoils included ammunition, mules, three wagons and two pieces of brass ordnance, now in the Tower of London. Prince Ferdinand of Brunswick, who witnessed the cavalry in action noted in orders: 'All the British Cavalry performed prodigies of valour.'

In October of 1760 the Tenth were again engaged in a sharp action when Lt.-Colonel Augustus Pitt was wounded and captured, soon to be exchanged and in command again. During 1761 and 1762, while brigaded with the Royal Horse Guards, 1st Dragoons and Scots Greys, they were frequently in action in the Bishopric of Paderborn and the Electorate of Hanover, until operations were finally suspended in 1762. After a final winter in Munster the Tenth returned to England in 1763 when a peace treaty was concluded and the Light Troop was disbanded. In 1764 the regiment was reviewed and favourably approved by King George III.

For the next sixteen years the regiment returned to its law and revenue enforcement duties at home, being stationed twice in Scotland and throughout various parts of England during that time. A notable promotion was that of Major Thomas Osbert Mordaunt to succeed Lt.-Colonel William Augustus Pitt in 1770. The two Mordaunts were

8

Army Museums Ogilby Trust

A private in the 10th Regiment of Dragoons.

thus serving as Lt.-Colonel and Colonel of the regiment for
ten years until General Sir John Mordaunt, K.B., died in
1780 after a Colonelcy of forty years, when he was succeeded by none other than Lt.-General Sir William
Augustus Pitt, K.B., whose long association with the regiment extended since he had joined as a cornet in 1744.

Chapter

2

B Y this time the experience gained in various wars had
fully confirmed the value of Light Dragoons and in
1783 the 7th, 9th, 10th, 11th, 13th and 14th Dragoons
were all formed into Light Dragoon regiments. An appropriate change of clothing and equipment was duly made,
but for the Tenth this was not all. Born in 1762, H.R.H.
George Augustus Frederick, Prince of Wales, had now
come of age and one of his healthier interests appears to
have been the Army. As a counter to his son's growing
friendship with Fox and his dissolute companions it is
understandable that George III wished to encourage this
interest, hence the following order from the Adjutant
General:

'29th September, 1783. ORDERS.

It is His Majesty's pleasure that the Tenth Regiment of
Light Dragoons shall, for the future, be called the "Tenth,
or Prince of Wales's Own Regiment of Light Dragoons."

William Fawcett. Adjutant General.'

This necessitated a further change of uniform the
following year from scarlet to blue and the Prince of Wales's
plume with the Rising Sun and Red Dragon became the
badges of the regiment, with the motto 'Ich Dien.' The
regiment was thenceforward much engaged in escort duties
to the royal family, being stationed mostly in the south
during this period and being several times reviewed by the
King, or members of the Royal Family. Thus it came about
that the Prince of Wales expressed a desire to be more
closely associated with the regiment and in 1793 was
appointed Colonel Commandant. The regiment was then
stationed at Brighton and Hounslow and in 1796 General

*H.R.H. George Augustus Frederick, Prince of Wales, Colonel of the
10th (Prince of Wales's Own) Royal Hussars.*

Sir William Augustus Pitt, K.B., was appointed to the
Colonelcy of the 1st Dragoon Guards and H.R.H. George
Augustus Frederick, Prince of Wales, was appointed
Colonel of the Regiment.

It followed naturally that his regiment had to be the

crack regiment in the British Army, first in valour, first in drill and manoeuvre, and, above all, first in appearance. To this end, as Colonel, he paid for specially tailored uniforms for the men to bring them all up to the standard of the uniforms worn by the N.C.O.s. To be an officer was a much sought after honour and it was typical of H.R.H. that in 1795 he gave a cornetcy in the regiment to his protege, then aged eighteen and recently heir to £30,000, later his friend and intimate for nearly twenty years, George 'Beau' Brummel.

Brummel, who progressed by purchase in three years to Captain, was no sort of a soldier at all, although soon arbiter of fashion in the civilian world. He was much away on leave as was often the custom then and never knew the names of the men in his troop, but always took his place on parade in front of an old soldier with a noticeably bulbous bottle nose. One day while he was absent on leave, his troop, being the junior one, was split up amongst the others to make up numbers. Brummel, arriving back late on parade as usual, could not find his blue-nosed soldier where he had expected him. Cantering up and down the ranks he found him at last and confidently took up his station in front of him.

'How now, Mr. Brummel? You are in the wrong troop,' the Colonel remonstrated.

'Oh no,' replied Brummel, turning round in his saddle. 'I know better than that; a pretty thing indeed if I did not know my own men.'

His military career was a short one. In 1798 the regiment was briefly posted to Manchester. This was too much for the Beau. He resigned his commission on the grounds that 'he was not prepared to go on foreign service'.

Much more admirable, if of a very different type, was the daredevil buck and gambler, Henry Mellish, who joined the Tenth from the Eleventh in 1798. Nearly six foot, weighing twelve stone, and extremely handsome, Henry Mellish was an accomplished musician and painter, an excellent pistol shot, a superb horseman and whip, as well as an athlete and sportsman with few equals in the country. So great was his extravagance on the racecourse and at the gambling tables, where on one occasion he lost £40,000 on a single throw of the dice (to H.R.H. his Colonel!), that he was granted perpetual leave lest he had an adverse effect on his brother officers. On one occasion he lost £97,000 in an evening, was persuaded to return and won back £100,000. It was only

Two corporals, a private and a trumpeter of the 10th Light Dragoons, circa 1793. Reproduced by gracious permission of Her Majesty the Queen.

after losing nearly all his money on the turf that he turned seriously to soldiering as an aide to Wellington, then Sir Arthur Wellesley, who observed that he had never seen a better or braver aide-de-camp than Captain Henry Mellish. It was only a pity that more of Prinny's friends were not cast in the same heroic mould.

In the meantime almost every European state had formed Hussar regiments in emulation of the renowned Hungarian light cavalry of that name. It is therefore not surprising to find at the Record Office the following entry made in 1803: 'Clothing Regulations: 22nd April, 1803. For the 10th Light Dragoons. Once every four years—1 pelisse, 1 dress-jacket, 1 hussar cap. Once every eight years—1 sash. Sd. Jas. Pulteney.'

With his regiment stationed at Brighton the Prince had clearly been unable to resist the temptation to dress them in the latest mode as Hussars, although the title was not as yet officially recognised in the British Army. It was not until 1806 that official sanction was obtained from George III to recognise and equip the regiment as Hussars, the first regiment in the British Army thus designated and equipped.

Shortly afterwards the 7th and 15th Light Dragoons were also converted to Hussars and similarly equipped with pelisses, sashes, fur caps, leather pantaloons and Hessian boots. Lighter carbines were also issued and both officers and men directed to grow moustaches. With two troops of Horse Artillery the three Hussar regiments were then formed in 1807 into the first Hussar brigade under the overall command of Major-General Lord Paget. Less felicitous was the choice of Brigadier-General John Slade, until 1798 second in command of the Tenth and a bosom friend of H.R.H. the Colonel, as Brigade commander. However it seems the Brigade soon learned new drill and movements which were carried out with great rapidity.

On October 17 and 18, 1808, on a war footing of eight

troops of eighty men each the 10th Hussars commanded by Lt.-Colonel Leigh embarked from Portsmouth for Corunna in the presence of their Royal Colonel. An emotional scene took place at the quayside when, after embracing his friend, 'His Royal Highness took off his sash and gave it to Brigadier-General Slade with his Hussar jacket and pellisse.' Unfortunately the ships were held in Stokes Bay by adverse winds until October 31, only arriving at Corunna on November 10, when the horses had to be swum ashore. Even so it was a further ten days before the rest of the divisions arrived and as it was with the preliminaries so it was with the campaign.

During that short and disastrous military operation, which started hesitantly against vastly superior numbers and ended as a rout, the Tenth were only engaged in three actions of any note, at Sahagun, at Mayorga and at Benevente. That they distinguished themselves at all was despite their Brigadier, whose name soon became a byword amongst the troops.

Captain Gordon of the 15th Hussars noted in his diary:

"Dec. 17th. We marched this day to Villa Graxima, which by the direct road is only three leagues from La Motta, but General Slade with his wonted sagacity contrived to find a route which increased the distance by two leagues . . . We had great reason on this occasion to lament the want of enterprise displayed by our worthy Brigadier and total neglect of all means to procure information: it was an unfortunate circumstance that he had chosen to attach himself to the 15th for if he had remained with the 10th I have little doubt that Colonel Grant (of the 15th) would have given us an opportunity of proving our mettle. . . ."

The action at Sahagun was planned as a simple encircling dawn attack, the Tenth under Slade to attack from one side and drive the French cavalry encamped there towards Lord Paget and the Fifteenth on the other side.

In the event the Fifteenth encountered the French with-
drawing and at once charged gallantly and routed them
completely. According to General Slade's diary: 'We
arrived . . . at the hour fixed, but the French were gone.
We followed through the town and found that the 15th
had not ten minutes charged and put them to rout. We
joined in the pursuit. . . .'

Captain Gordon tells a different story:

> 'Dec. 21st. General Slade was directed to attack the
> convent with the 10th. . . . This plan however was
> rendered abortive by the bad state of the roads and the
> dilatory proceedings of the Brigadier, who . . . made a
> long speech to the troops, which he concluded with the
> energetic peroration of "Blood and Slaughter—March!"
> . . . If General Slade had sent forward an officer to
> announce his approach, *or if he had joined in the pursuit*
> . . . not a single Frenchman would have escaped.'

Captain Gordon was an eyewitness of the action at
Mayorga:

> '. . . two squadrons of chasseurs à cheval were dis-
> covered on rising ground about a mile distant. Lord
> Paget directed General Slade to attack them with a
> squadron of the 10th supported by the remainder of the
> regiment. The General moved off at a trot, but had not
> advanced far when he halted to have some alterations
> made in the length of his stirrups. An aide-de-camp was
> sent to enquire the cause of the delay and the squadron
> was again put in motion, but the General's stirrups were
> not yet adjusted to his mind and he halted again before
> they had advanced a hundred yards. Lord Paget, whose
> patience was this time quite exhausted, then ordered
> Colonel Leigh to take the lead. The 10th charged
> gallantly, routed the enemy, and took between forty and
> fifty prisoners with little loss on their part.'

At Benevente on December 29 the 10th Hussars were
fortunately under the direct command of Lord Paget. A

16

Private Grisdall captures General Desnouettes at Benevente.

force of about 600 French cavalry of the Imperial Guard
had crossed the fords of the river Esla and were driving
back the piquets on the plain. The 10th Hussars, with the
7th Hussars in reserve, were waiting concealed by some
houses. Ordered to charge, they galloped forward at full
speed. The piquets joined in the attack and the French
turned and fled for the river, losing seventy prisoners and
130 killed and wounded.

Amongst the prisoners was General Lefevre-Desnouettes,
who on refusing to halt, was wounded and captured by
Private Levi Grisdall of the Tenth. The General was
commander in chief of the French cavalry and his capture
at this stage may well have caused sufficient confusion
amongst the French command to delay their advance, at a
highly critical time in the British Army's retreat. Private
Grisdall was subsequently promoted to sergeant by order
of the Prince Regent.

From January 14 to 17 the British Army was evacuated

by sea from Corunna and the miserable campaign was crowned by the death of Sir John Moore in action on the 16th. After shooting most of their horses to prevent them falling into the hands of the French the cavalry regiments embarked on the 15th and 16th. The Tenth, who had embarked from England with 600 horses in October, 1808, arrived back at Brighton in February, 1809, with only thirty. For their conduct on foreign service however the regiment received the thanks of H.R.H. the Prince of Wales on their return and again later at a review in August at Brighton.

During 1809 and 1810 their losses were replaced and the regiment was commended once again on its appearance, at one review by the Duke of York and at another by the Prince of Wales. In 1810 Lt.-Colonel George Leigh retired from the army. He was succeeded by Lt.-Colonel George Quentin, a Frenchman by birth, who had first joined the regiment in 1794 and served as riding master, in which capacity he became a close friend of the Prince.

In 1811, during the temporary derangement of George III, the Prince of Wales became Prince Regent and one of his first acts was to confer the distinguished title 'Royal' on his regiment, which thus became 'The Tenth, the Prince of Wales's Own, Royal Regiment of Hussars'. Unofficially they appear to have been known at this time as 'The Tenth, the Prince Regent's Own, Royal Regiment of Hussars'. He also seems to have taken the opportunity of issuing an order dated retrospectively to 1807 officially clothing and equipping the Hussar Brigade as Hussars.

While stationed at Brighton during this period the Prince and the officers of the Tenth often rode on the downs. Out with the Royal beagles on horseback one afternoon all efforts to find a hare failed and extempore races over sheep hurdles were arranged instead. These proved successful and it is said were the first introduction of hurdle racing in this country.

In the meantime Captain Henry Mellish of the Tenth had so distinguished himself that he had been promoted Colonel and Assistant Adjutant-General on Wellington's staff. During the battle of Busaco Napoleon's General Massena had been so impressed by the 'behaviour of the officer he had seen riding coolly about his duties that when Mellish was sent under a flag of truce to arrange terms for the wounded he asked him to dine to make his acquaintance.' On another occasion it was reported to Wellington that he had been captured by the French.

'They won't keep him long,' was his prophecy.

Lt.-Colonel Henry Mellish, 10th Hussars.

Sure enough, next day he was seen riding into camp mounted on a shaggy Iberian donkey. This caused laughter amongst his brother officers, who declared it was not worth £5.

'I'll make it worth £35 before long,' he replied confidently, duly accepting a considerable wager on this score.

Thereupon he rode it straight at the enemy lines until it was shot under him. He then returned and successfully claimed the £35 government compensation for the loss of an officer's charger, as well as the sum due on his wager. As Assistant Adjutant-General to Wellington he was one of the few people entrusted with the writing of despatches. It was thus only his due when he was appointed Equerry to H.R.H. the Prince of Wales in 1812.

In the same year, 1812, during the absence of the Life Guards in the Peninsula, the regiment was quartered in the

Army Museums Ogilby Trust

10th Hussars in camp, 1813.

10 H.—2

Knightsbridge barracks. While there they themselves received orders to prepare for active service on the Peninsula. Lt.-Colonel Quentin was at this time suffering from a ruptured blood vessel and was under doctor's orders, so that the six service troops embarked at Portsmouth under Lt.-Colonel Palmer, the junior Lt.-Colonel, and landed at Lisbon in February 1813. Formed into Brigade with the Fifteenth and Eighteenth Hussars they were at first under the command of the senior major, Major Robarts, as Lt.-Colonel Palmer had to return to England on urgent business.

After one or two minor skirmishes the Tenth were in the van of the Brigade near Morales on June 2, when they encountered a considerable body of French cavalry formed in two lines in battle order. Led by Major Robarts, the Tenth, supported by the Eighteenth with the Fifteenth in reserve, charged the enemy overthrowing the first line then breaking through the second line as well and going on to pursue them two miles. Two officers and two hundred men were captured with the loss of only one officer and one private killed and one officer, two N.C.O.s and ten privates wounded or missing. Wellington wrote:

> 'The Tenth have had a very handsome affair. . . . Their loss is small, but they must have destroyed the enemy's Sixteenth dragoons.'

His despatch concluded:

> ' . . . this gallant affair . . . reflects great credit upon Major Robarts and the Tenth Hussars.'

During the rest of the month of June the Tenth further distinguished themselves whenever engaged with the enemy, especially at Vittoria, where the left squadron under Captain Wyndham seized the French baggage, consisting of over 143 cannon, ammunition and loot, in the face of a column of infantry on one side and a body of French cavalry on the other. The regiment speedily rallied to them and first forced the French dragoons to retreat then turned on the infantry who hastily withdrew. The Tenth then pursued the French rearguard along the road to Pampeluna until sunset, Captain Wyndham's squadron capturing Joseph Buonaparte's carriage and forcing him to take to horseback in the nick of time.

In July, during the blockade of Pampeluna, they remained in reserve at the foot of Pyrénées, providing patrols in the battles of the Pyrénées, but without real scope for cavalry action. It was then, apparently still suffering from the effects of another ruptured blood vessel and acting against the express advice of his doctors, but no doubt spurred by reports of the regiment's victories, that Lt.-Colonel Quentin arrived from England. It was no time for a sick man with little experience of active service to be in command and the immediate result was a rapid deterioration in the regimental spirit and discipline.

In December, following the advance of the Army, the Tenth entered France across the Pyrénées. In January and February they were engaged in patrolling the front. In February, after the battle of Orthez, in which they had been able to take little part due to the nature of the ground, the right squadron under Lt.-Colonel Palmer was in pursuit of the retreating enemy rearguard when they encountered a body of French cavalry. One troop was dispersed as skirmishers, but Lt.-Colonel Palmer at once charged at the head of the reserve troop and broke the enemy, killing several and taking thirty-four dragoons prisoner.

By this time matters in the regiment had reached the point where General Lord Combermere, the cavalry commander, later admitted his intention of asking to have Lt.-Colonel Quentin relieved as 'unfit to command a regiment of light cavalry on active service.' As the war was nearing its end he contented himself on March 30 by ordering the Brigade Commander, Lord Somerset, to read a letter from the Adjutant-General to the assembled officers of the regiment. The following is an extract:

'Adjutant General to Lord Somerset commanding Hussar Brigade:

'I am commanded by my Lord Wellington to take this occasion of mentioning that the complaints against the 10th Hussars are so general and so extremely discreditable to the regiment and prejudicial to the interests of the army, it is requisite you should immediately adopt measures to re-establish that discipline which is necessary to good order, but which has been allowed to relax to an unpardonable degree under the command of Lt.-Colonel Quentin.

'Your Lordship will be so good as to communicate to the Lt.-Colonel the Field Marshal's displeasure at having to notice irregularities it was in his power to have prevented; and that a recurrence of such breach of regulations and good order, will convince his Excellency that the Lt.-Colonel is unequal to the command of a regiment of the first pretensions.'

The next major action, the battle of Toulouse, on April 12, proved to be the last of the war and gave little scope for cavalry, although the regiment suffered several casualties from a severe cannonading they were forced to endure. The abdication of Napoleon followed soon afterwards and hostilities ceased on April 18. Preparations were at once made for returning home, and during these the regiment learned that it had been awarded the honour of bearing 'Peninsula' on its appointments in recognition of its services during the campaigns of 1809 and 1813–14. By way of Boulogne they then embarked for England, returning to Brighton on July 24.

It was only then that the feelings of the officers, which must have been simmering for a long time, finally reached boiling point. All twenty-four officers who had fought in the campaign, excepting those most recently joined from England, sent a signed letter through Lt.-Colonel Palmer to H.R.H. their Colonel. Its terms were deplorably vague, but it was virtually an invitation to him to dismiss his friend Quentin.

Those were the days of political intrigue and many of the officers were from families wielding considerable political power. The senior officers involved, Major Robarts and Lt.-Colonel Palmer, both subsequently entered Parliament, but whether any of them were indeed moved by anything more than honest if inarticulate indignation is doubtful. H.R.H.'s reaction to the letter was to demand to know what charges they wished to bring against Quentin. In another extremely involved letter they indicated that they had no wish for a court-martial, but that it was a matter for him to decide. Thereafter one senses H.R.H.'s master hand at work behind the scenes.

Lt.-Colonel Quentin demanded a court martial. He was charged rather loosely on three counts of failing to lead his men, i.e. of cowardice, and one of allowing slackness of discipline leading to the reprimand already noted. Surprisingly Lt.-Colonel Palmer was chosen as Prosecutor. The proceedings were of considerable interest and it was obvious from Lord Combermere and Lord Somerset's evidence alone that Quentin had been unfit to command, even if the other evidence had not been conclusive. The list of punishments awarded to the regiment at this period makes horrific reading today. However H.R.H. was looking after his friend and Quentin was duly acquitted.

It was in the solution to the problem this acquittal presented that H.R.H.'s manipulation became most apparent. It was clearly certain to bring about a storm of protest if all the signatories of the letter were to be cashiered or court-martialled in their turn. They belonged to some of the most influential families in the land, among them the Marquis of Worcester, two Fitzclarences, grandsons of the Duke of Clarence, Lord Hill and the Duc de Guiche. Moreover they had almost all served with distinction and honour in the recent campaign. However H.R.H. was equal to the situation. Lt.-Colonel Quentin remained in command of the regiment and the three officers who had not signed the letter also remained with the regiment. The rest were dispersed amongst other cavalry regiments and the required number of replacements extracted in their stead. These officers thus became widely known as 'The Elegant Extracts,' but so fitting a phrase was inevitably applied to them all, incomers and outgoers alike.

One obvious and looked for result was a duel between Quentin and Palmer. Early in January 1815 Quentin went to Paris, where he had heard Palmer was staying, with the intention of challenging him there, since the rules against

Sword exercises: 'Cut two, against infantry'.

duelling were strict in England. Palmer was in Bordeaux and Quentin had to wait until February before issuing his challenge. Despite many letters urging him not to accept, on the grounds that he had merely been executing his public duty, Palmer duly accepted. The Duc de Guiche, lately Captain de Grammont of the Tenth, who felt very strongly on the issue, wished to act as Palmer's second, but was refused in order to avoid implicating him. They met. Lt.-Colonel Quentin fired first at twelve paces and missed his man. Lt.-Colonel Palmer, to show he had no private motive, then fired in the air and both parties duly declared themselves satisfied.

Chapter
3

IN September of 1814 the Tenth left Brighton and were
stationed in Romford in Essex. During March 1815 they
were briefly in London, helping to suppress the
riots following the introduction of the unpopular Corn
Laws. Then came news of Napoleon's return to France
and the six troops of the regiment were embarked at
Ramsgate in April, landing at Ostend on the 17th and
18th.

They were at first again brigaded with the Seventh and
the Eighteenth Hussars, but in the rapid re-organisation of
the Anglo-Allied Army the Seventh were soon replaced by
the First King's German Hussars. Their brigade Commander was General Sir Hussey Vivian and in the seven
cavalry brigades of the Anglo-Allied Army under the Earl
of Uxbridge this Hussar brigade was numbered sixth. On
June 2 the Tenth and Eighteenth gave a farewell race
meeting and fête, near Grammont, to the Seventh Hussars
on their departure to another brigade.

On June 15 Napoleon crossed the frontier. The Tenth
received their orders in the early hours of the following
morning and were soon on the move. After an approach
march of over fifty miles in bad going they arrived that
evening on the scene of the battle which had taken place
near Quatre Bras, after the action was over. They stood to
arms all night and the following morning, of the 17th,
Captain Grey's troop was sent to get in touch with the
Prussians, which was successfully accomplished. During
the day the British Army fell back eight miles on Waterloo,
covered by the cavalry, the Tenth being engaged mounted
and dismounted against the enemy.

That night the Tenth were bivouacked in torrential rain
close to Waterloo. In the morning of the 18th the rain
stopped and Vivian's brigade was posted on the extreme
left of the entire Army. Major Taylor was sent out with a
patrol to cover the left flank and to try to get in touch with
the Prussians, which he succeeded in doing, bringing back
the important news that General Von Bulow was marching
to the assistance of the British.

The French attack began about 11 a.m. and the firing
soon became heavy. Shortly after noon the Earl of Uxbridge
committed the Heavy Brigades to the attack, losing a great
part of the British cavalry in the process and leaving
Wellington with little reserve. Meanwhile Vivian had
moved his brigade to the right, lining them up behind two
regiments of Brunswick infantry, thus both supporting them
and preventing their further retreat. Here Lt.-Colonel
Quentin was shot in the foot and command of the Tenth
then devolved on Lt.-Colonel Lord Robert Manners. The
regiment continued patiently to withstand some galling fire
for nearly two hours.

In the evening the news of the Prussians' arrival meant
that at last the left flank was covered. Wellington ordered
Vivian to attack the enemy cavalry near *La Belle Alliance*.
The cavalry were Cuirassiers, i.e. in armour, supported by
eight squares of the famed Imperial Old Guard, the
Emperor's foremost infantry. In order to outflank them,
Vivian ordered the advance by column of half squadrons
before ordering 'line to the front by order of Regiments'
with the Tenth in the lead.

As soon as the first squadron was formed Vivian sounded
the charge and so great was the pace that the charge was in
echelon with the Cuirassiers in full flight before the left
squadron of the Tenth was in action. Vivian then sounded
the halt and rally, but only half the right squadron under
Major Howard heard. They rallied to Vivian who ordered
them to attack a nearby square of infantry. Major Howard

charged to his death at the head of the half squadron and the square was driven back into retreat.

Meanwhile the rest of the Tenth under Lord Manners charged on, driving the Cuiraissiers before them, until they encountered a battalion of the French Old Imperial Guard with cavalry in support of them. Lord Manners rallied the regiment under their fire and then charged, putting the Imperial Guard and cavalry to flight. With the Imperial Guard on the run a general panic ensued, so that it was the gallant charge of the Tenth that finally decided the day.

Let some of the Tenth who were present on that day speak for themselves. Captain Charles Wood, wounded by a ball in the thigh, wrote from Brussels:

> 'You should have seen us all the night before the fight. Everyone wet through. We had a shower that came down like a wall. Our horses could not face it and all went about. It made the ground up to the horses' fetlocks. We got into a small cottage close to our bivouac about a mile in the rear of the position, most of us naked and getting our things dry by the fire. . . . Old Quentin burnt his boots and could not get them on. . . . We had to feed on what we found in the hut, beginning with the old hens for supper and the young chickens for breakfast. I see the English papers say, "The light Dragoons could make no impression on the French Cuirassiers." Now our regiment actually rode over them. Give me the boys that will go at a swinging gallop for the last seventy yards applying both spurs when you come within the last six yards. Then if you don't go right over them I am much mistaken. . . .'

Private Marshall of the Tenth writing home described the end of the day thus:

> 'At length we assembled what few we had got together of the regiment and the General (Vivian) addressed us: "Now Tenth," he said. "You have not disappointed me; you are just what I thought you were; you were the first regiment that broke their lines and to you it is we are

indebted for turning the fate of the day and depend upon it your Prince shall know it, for nothing but the bravery and discipline of the regiment could have completed such a work." We then gave him three cheers.'

William Cartwright, then a Lieutenant in the Tenth, aged 18, later General William Cartwright, wrote:

'My dear Father,   Waterloo, 19th June.

Although I have seen many battles in my life, I assure you they were a complete farce to the one for this last three days. Bony, against us, fought like a tiger; we fought like Englishmen and thanks to God, repelled him with great loss. Our cavalry behaved so finely that every-one when they saw us was quite thunderstruck. I only wonder we were not all killed. Thank God, I have been

The silver trumpet commemorating Waterloo.

lucky enough to escape. I commanded a troop on this
occasion. We charged four or five times our number—
the men in armour—but we made a pretty hole in them;
there are not above six officers left with the Regiment.
I command a squadron now. We have been fighing
since the 16th. I will give you another letter in a day or
two, but in the meantime please excuse this scrawl. We
are within three leagues of Brussels. In haste, etc. Your
most affectionate son.'

Surprisingly enough the regimental losses at Waterloo
were not as great as might have been expected, being only
two officers, nineteen men and fifty-one horses killed, six
officers, one N.C.O., twenty-four men and a trumpeter
wounded and thirteen horses missing. In commemoration
of the battle a silver medal was struck and bestowed on all
ranks and the word 'Waterloo' was added to the regimental
battle honours. A silver trumpet, now in the Officer's Mess
bears the following inscription:

Purchased
By Desire of The
Soldiers of the Tenth or Prince Regent's
Own Royal Hussars
With Part of the Prize Money
Arising from the Enemy's Horses
Captured by Their Brigade
Under the Command Of
Major General Sir H. Vivian, K.C.B.
At the Battle Of
Waterloo
18 June 1815

After Waterloo the regiment followed the retreating
French forces to Paris, capturing General Lauriston, one of
Napoleon's aides-de-camp on the way, as he was in the act
of changing sides. Paris capitulated on July 4 and a rather
uneasy occupation followed the restoration of the Bour-

bons, during which the Tenth were initially stationed in very comfortable quarters at Beauvais, before moving eventually to Boulogne.

While at Beauvais Captain Bacon of the Tenth, later a General in the Portuguese Army, introduced stage coaches and four in hand teams in Paris, where they used to meet regularly. At a time when duels seem to have been an everyday occurrence with ex-Napoleonic officers going out of their way to pick quarrels with members of the Allied or Bourbon forces he also seems to have been involved in a somewhat unusual duel. In this instance the Frenchman refused to fight with pistols. Bacon refused to fight with swords. They finally compromised by fighting on horseback with lances, when Bacon after being twice wounded eventually killed his man.

In January the Tenth left Calais for England, being nearly shipwrecked on the Goodwins and losing thirty-six horses overboard before arriving back at Brighton. Here they promptly found themselves back at their familiar peace-time duties of revenue enforcement in the Hastings and Worthing area, where smuggling was rampant, later detaching squadrons to the West Country for the same purpose. They were also engaged in review duty and appearances at court.

During 1819 and 1820 they returned to Scotland for a duty tour. Their uniform at this time was an eyecatching spectacle, described in the Army List as follows: 'A shako, larger in circumference at the top than the bottom, made of blue cloth (previously red) with an upright feather, or plume, and gold lace. Pelisse blue, with black fur. Jacket blue, with cross loops and olivets in gold, blue facings. Girdle, crimson and gold. Trousers, blue with double gold stripe.' Leopard skins were also carried on the saddles of officers, with shell ornaments, which had first been introduced in 1812 purely for reviews, on the bridles, breast plates and cruppers. In addition the officers wore chain belts, the latter supposedly giving rise to one of the many nick-names of the regiment, 'The Chainy Tenth.'

By this time H.R.H. George Augustus Frederick, Prince of Wales, had been associated with the regiment as Commandant and Colonel for twenty-seven years and it had attained all his highest aspirations. It had proved its valour, it was superb in drill and manoeuvre and without equal in appearance. No-one could ask for more, even H.R.H. Then in 1820 George III died and he finally became George IV. Automatically the Colonelcy fell vacant. It was conferred on Lt.-General Charles William Vane, Lord Stewart, afterwards Marquis of Londonderry.

Meanwhile the Tenth were having an active time in Scotland. Centred on Edinburgh they had troops stationed at Forfar, Perth, Stirling and Glasgow. There were however continual riots amongst the weavers in Glasgow and Paisley and more troops had to be sent there. Then there was a report of an armed band of nineteen men intercepting the mail near Kilsyth. These were cornered on Bonnymuir by Lt. Hodgson with Sergeant Saxelby and nine men of the Tenth accompanied by nine Yeomanry. They received their fire and charged them sword in hand, making them all prisoners, but not before Hodgson had his horse shot under him and a pike wound in the hand and Sergeant Saxelby two pike wounds in the side. No doubt they were quite glad to return south to Hounslow once more, to be reviewed by King George IV and in 1821 to be present at his coronation, before finally returning to their old quarters in Brighton.

In 1822, after a review on Hounslow Heath by the Duke of York, a banquet was held in London by the Colonel of the Tenth, the Marquis of Londonderry. On behalf of His Majesty he presented the regiment with a magnificent silver-gilt centre-piece 'as a memorial of his favourable sentiments towards the corps he had commanded from the year 1793 till his accession to the throne in 1820.' The

centre-piece consists of a large pedestal surrounded by
candelabra, with

engraved on one panel:	on another panel:
The Gift of	
His Majesty	Benevente
KING GEORGE IV	Corunna
To The	Morales del Toro
10th, or Prince of Wales's	Vittoria
Own Royal Regiment	Orthez
Which He Commanded	Toulouse
From The Year 1793	Waterloo
Until His Accession	
To The Throne	

On a third panel is the Prince of Wales's plume. Each
corner is adorned with an allegorical figure, the whole
supporting a statuette of George IV dressed as a Roman
Emperor. To supplement this royal present the Colonel
presented the regiment with two large richly embossed
silver-gilt soup toureens. These, with other gifts form part
of the officer's mess gold plate.

In the same year the regiment embarked for Ireland,
landing at Waterford and being first based at Cahir before
moving to Dublin the following year. This was the regiment's first visit to Dublin and their appearance and bearing caused much admiring and humorous comment. It is
said that to avoid introductions at a ball given by the Lord
Mayor of Dublin the officers of the Tenth who attended
declared 'The Tenth don't dance,' which soon became a
popular sarcasm. It was then they received the nickname
'The China Tenth,' as supposedly being precious enough
to require the same care as delicate china, also, more
obviously, 'The Shiny Tenth' because of their glittering
appearance. This in due course became shortened to 'The
Shiners' and was proudly adopted by the Tenth as implying
outshone by none.

In 1824 Colonel Sir George Quentin retired from command. It may have been then that the popular regimental saying 'Once a Tenth Hussar, always a Tenth Hussar' arose, because his successor was none other than Lt.-Colonel Henry Wyndham, one of the original 'Elegant Extracts,' who had seized the baggage at Vittoria. Shortly after his appointment the regiment was reviewed at Phoenix Park by Lord Londonderry accompanied by Lady Londonderry, both in the uniform of the Tenth, but the latter wearing a busby although the regiment wore shakos.

During this visit a certain Cornet Battier considered himself aggrieved when a decision in the Mess referred to Lord Londonderry was taken against him. He transferred to the infantry and then to half-pay, carrying on an acrimonious correspondence and ending up by publicly accusing Lord Londonderry of 'sheltering behind his rank.' A duel ensued at ten paces when Lord Londonderry missed and Mr. Battier's pistol misfired. Lord Londonderry promptly requested him to have another shot, but his second declined and from the shooting viewpoint the matter ended, but that was by no means the end of the affair.

The Duke of York issued a General Order of which part expressed: 'His Majesty's concern and displeasure that an officer of Lord Londonderry's high rank and military reputation should have committed himself in personal collision with an inferior officer by accepting a challenge from any supposed aggression proceeding from the exercise of his authority as colonel.' The *Gazette* announced the name of Mr. Battier erased from the half-pay list and he was horsewhipped by Sir Henry Hardinge, Secretary to the Ordnance.

The Duke of Wellington, with his usual commonsense, thought it 'unnecessary for his Royal Highness to take any notice' and in a letter to Lord Londonderry starting 'My dear Charles' he wrote:

'Your mistake is one which has crept into the service lately and is very general. It is in supposing the mess anything but a private society. . . . In truth Mr. Battier was a member of the mess as long as he was at quarters with the regiment and paid part of the expenses of the very dinner given to you, not a member, but a stranger, and unless you make the mess something more than a private society, I don't see what business you, as colonel, had to notice his presence there.

'The whole case is unfortunate. It is in everybody's mouth, in all the newspapers, and in the theatres, and the Hussars are very ill-treated. I see that they now want to get them out of Dublin; but I have entreated his Royal Highness to keep them there the full time, although I think it is not impossible they may have to fight a duel or two. But that I consider of no consequence. . . .'

The Duke of York did not take Wellington's advice. The Tenth left Dublin and for the rest of their stay in Ireland were stationed at Ballinrobe. Whether any duels ensued is not recorded. The rest of their tour of duty seems to have been uneventful.

In 1825 they returned to England via Bristol, where they were promptly engaged in suppressing rioting weavers, before going on to revenue enforcement duties in the West Country. They had moved on to Northampton in 1826 when Portugal was threatened by Spanish invasion. An expeditionary force was promptly prepared, including two squadrons of the 10th Hussars and two of the 12th Lancers brigaded under Colonel Wyndham, which embarked in 1827. Their appearance was enough to cause the Spanish to withdraw, but they remained there until 1828. Then the Tenth returned to their old quarters at Brighton and in 1829 were inspected by the Duke of Orleans at a grand review in Hyde Park when they were commanded in person by Lord Londonderry.

It must have seemed the old familiar routine, but next

year found them in Yorkshire, based on Leeds, nor were they to return to Brighton for forty years. In 1830 their royal patron George IV died and was succeeded by William IV. The chill wind of change seems to have been felt at once. An immediate result was an order in 1831: 'The four regiments of hussars to be dressed perfectly alike. Their officers to have one dress only and that of a less costly pattern, which will forthwith be prepared.' The last part of this order does not seem to have been carried out, but there were no more exclusive royal reviews, no more pleasant sojourns in Brighton, no more court functions. The Tenth were back to reality again. It was the end of an era. Soon after this order was issued the Tenth were on their way to Ireland again, to be stationed in Dublin.

Chapter

4

DESPITE having to enforce the First Coercion Act the regiment seems to have settled down in Ireland again more happily than on their first visit and their tour of duty passed without particular incident. The fact that in 1832 Major Lord Thomas Cecil of the Tenth won the Grand Military Steeplechase on Lt. the Hon. H. Saville's mare Modesty may have had more than a little to do with it. The Irish have always admired a good horse and a good horseman and the Tenth was short of neither.

In 1836 the Tenth moved to Scotland and after a brief spell in Glasgow and Hamilton returned to Yorkshire, where in 1837 they heard of the death of William IV and the accession of Queen Victoria. The following year found them back at Hounslow acting as royal escorts once again and they were amongst the troops present at the coronation and a grand review shortly afterwards. From there they were posted to the West Country to assist in controlling the serious Chartist riots of 1839, which were particularly bad in Newport, where they had to fire on the rioting mob.

Their next move took them to Northampton, where the first Grand Military Steeplechase was held that year (1840), and to the regiment's satisfaction the adjutant Sir James Baird won the first gold cup on his brown mare Carlow. However they were only stationed at Northampton a year when O'Connell's efforts in Ireland to repeal the Union resulted in them being posted back to Dublin because of the general unrest in the country.

At this time Lord and Lady Londonderry were much in attendance on Queen Victoria and, remembering Lady Londonderry's preference for the busby rather than the shako, it is possible to detect a slightly sour note in a letter from the Adjutant General addressed to 'General the Marquis of Londonderry, Colonel of the 10th Hussars.' It read:

'Horse Guards: 6th August, 1841.

Sir—By request of the General Commanding-in-Chief, I have the honour to acquaint your Lordship that her Majesty has been graciously pleased to approve of the 10th, or the Prince of Wales's Own Royal Dragoons (Hussars), resuming the fur hussar cap formerly worn by the regiment.—I have &c. Signed A. G. Macdonald. A.G.'

In 1842 the busby duly replaced the shako, which the Tenth and other Hussar regiments had been wearing in various shapes and sizes since 1822. In the same year the regiment moved from Dublin to Ballincolig and from thence to Cahir. Then Lord Londonderry was transferred from the Colonelcy of the 10th Hussars to that of the 2nd Life Guards. He was replaced by Major-General the Hon. Beauchamp Lygon, later Earl Beauchamp.

The Tenth's tour of duty in Ireland passed fairly un-eventfully for the next three years and in 1845 they returned to England, being posted to York. At that time there was no hint of any special further move. Then, like a bombshell, came the announcement that they must prepare for service in India, their first overseas posting to a tropical climate. In those days such a posting entailed great changes. Officers who could not afford a Hussar regiment at home were able to afford it in India, where living costs were much lower, and many officers who were prepared to serve at home were unable or unwilling to face the hazards of the climate in India. At the same time the establishment was increased from six troops to nine. The result was a quite startling difference in the list of officers, nearly equivalent to that after the exchange of 'The Elegant Extracts,' but, as then, the spirit of the Tenth remained unchanged.

In order to bring the regiment up to the full strength of the new establishment in a short time, drafts of volunteers had to be obtained from other cavalry regiments, amongst which were the Royal Dragoons, the Scots Greys, the 7th, 8th and 11th Hussars. The Tenth was largely composed of picked men whose average height then was 5 feet 9½ inches, remarkably tall for light cavalry, and the volunteers who joined them were well matched. Thus when Sir George Brown, the Adjutant General, inspected the regiment before it embarked he remarked that they more resembled Lifeguards than Hussars.

Embarking in May in three separate ships from Gravesend, they arrived at Bombay, via the Cape, before the end of August. They then marched to their cavalry station at Kirkee, the journey taking ten days and being notable for three deaths from cholera, en route. Fortunately the disease

The 10th Hussars at Kirkee.

did not spread further, for it was the scourge of the British soldier in India at that time.

The regiment was also fortunate in taking over one of the healthiest stations in the country, which for many years had been occupied by the 4th and subsequently the 14th Light Dragoons, for this was to be their home for the next eight years. Their first problem was to secure horses and after a seven month period of dismounted training they obtained a batch of remounts of pure Arab or Persian stock. Although small, these proved extremely hardy, full of spirit and yet very amenable to training, but being all stallions they often caused trouble by biting and kicking one another. The rule in India however was one man, one horse, from which he was never parted unless necessary on good grounds and both officers and men became extremely fond of them.

In the Dress Regulations for 1846 the dress of the 10th Hussars was:

'Busby—Nine inches deep and the same size at the top as the bottom. Scarlet fly and plaited top.

Plume—White egret with scarlet bottom.

Trousers—Blue cloth with a stripe of gold lace one inch and a half wide down the outward seam. (The 10th and 11th Hussars are permitted to wear two stripes of gold lace each three-quarters of an inch wide with a light between.)

Pouch belt—The 10th Hussars are permitted to wear, both in dress and undress, a pouch and pouch belt of black patent leather according to regimental pattern.

Undress Belts and Slings—10th Hussars' Russian leather.'

Not surprisingly, this was found unsuitable for India. The busby was replaced with a shako and the regiment provided with white cotton clothing for ordinary wear. This consisted of a stable jacket and overalls of cotton twill and a white cotton quilted cover worn on the shako with a curtain hanging down to cover the temples as well as the back of the head and neck.

In those days it was not only the climate, but the monotony of life in a regimental station in India that proved irksome. Private William Douglas of the Tenth, who assisted Colonel R. S. Liddell with an earlier regimental history, gives a very clear picture of this in a book entitled appropriately *Soldiering in Sunshine and Storm*, which he wrote subsequently 'under great difficulties' in the barracks at Cahir in 1864.

The officers did their best to alleviate the monotony. Cricket, fives and other games were organized, a dramatic society was formed and the bandsmen of the Tenth particularly proved themselves excellent actors and comedians. The Tenth's theatre became a recognised attraction, as did the annual balls, dinners and similar festivities of the 'season.' Strive as they might however the monotony remained, much aggravated by the climate and occasional outbreaks of cholera.

Five years passed thus uneventfully at Kirkee until rumours of the impending war in the Crimea started in 1853. When war broke out in 1854 the Tenth were keyed to the highest pitch of expectation, daily awaiting the call to action, only to have their hopes dashed. Private Douglas described how, during a critical point in a needle cricket match in July 1854, Colonel Parlby suddenly galloped onto the pitch waving despatches announcing that the regiment was under orders for the Crimea. The news was received with delighted cheers and the match was forgotten, but unfortunately the news was soon countermanded. It was only after the famous and ill-fated charge at Balaclava in October had decimated the light cavalry that the regiment finally entrained for Bombay and thence shipped to Suez early in 1855.

From Suez in the days before the canal it was necessary to march over the desert to Cairo. In order to avoid the heat of the day the marches were made at night and it proved a wearisome, if well managed, four day trek. On arrival at Cairo a six week wait ensued, but as the Crimea operations were such that no cavalry was involved, no one objected to the delay, which was put to good use in training fresh remounts and similar work.

Eventually another march of ten days over very difficult going took the regiment to Alexandria. The march was enlivened by the appearance of an arab sheik, who claimed to own the fastest horse in the desert and challenged the regiment to match a horse against it over any distance. A match and wager was agreed and the regiment's fastest horse and rider chosen, but when the sheik's horse appeared it was obvious that it was only just 'up from grass' and completely out of condition. Although it made a good start it could not stay the pace and never really stood a chance. The wager of £30 was duly paid, but the sheik, no longer the proud owner of the fastest horse in the desert, went off dejected.

From Alexandria the Tenth sailed for Balaclava and 109 days after leaving India finally reached the Crimea. From the moment they had received orders to embark Colonel Parlby had abolished pipe clay and shaving and the men in buff belts, slings and gloves, bronzed and bearded, on their fine Arab horses apparently made a great impression on everyone who saw them. *The Times* correspondent wrote: 'The Tenth Hussars were conspicuous for the soldierly, efficient look of the men and the fine condition of their light, sinewy and showy horses.' The horses gained a particularly evil reputation for their 'aggressive propensities' often getting loose and chasing riders on the road to the front, which ran close to the camp, 'regardless of person or rank'.

The Tenth, over 600 sabres strong, turned out on the first morning of their arrival owing to an anticipated Russian advance, which never materialized. The following day they took part in a reconnaissance towards the Tchernaya. Thereafter they were very fully occupied in reconnaissance, outpost duties, convoy and orderly work, for, until the arrival of the 12th Lancers from India and remounts from England, they were virtually the only effective cavalry available.

On May 25 the 10th Hussars with the 12th Lancers and two troops of the R.H.A. under Colonel Parlby acted as covering troops for the allied force occupying the line of the Tchernaya, which they had already reconnoitred. Thereafter the regiment split into two wings, one with Colonel Wilkie in the force under General De La Marmora acting as outlying pickets at night and patrols during the day, the other under Colonel Parlby with the main army. Reunited again, the regiment was further employed in reconnaissance work under Osman Pasha when an outbreak of cholera caused nine deaths.

In August the Russians attacked the Tchernaya line, but the French General Pelissier refused to allow the combined French and English cavalry to attack the guns, no doubt remembering the tragedy at Balaclava, although in this case there were 6,000 Light and Heavy cavalry eager to charge and the outcome would have been very different. Nor were the cavalry employed at the siege of Sebastopol in September, when the infantry were repulsed in a day of bloody carnage, although after their stubborn resistance the Russians withdrew in the night leaving the battered town to the allies.

A squadron of the Tenth with a squadron of the Chasseurs d'Afrique embarked to support a force under General Sir George Brown, which had captured Kertch. During this expedition a troop under Captain Clarke was cut off by a force of 300 Cossacks while engaged on reconnaissance. They charged the centre of the enemy in spite of a volley of fire and cut their way through, making good their retreat, with the loss of two privates killed and one sergeant-major, one farrier and fourteen men missing. Further actions followed and this squadron operated at Kertch throughout the winter.

The rest of the Tenth wintered in Turkey at Ismid on the Sea of Marmora in pleasant winter quarters until peace was proclaimed early in 1856. There followed a painful parting with the Arab horses which were given to the Turkish government. The regiment then embarked for Portsmouth, where they arrived on June 28 after foreign service lasting just over ten years.

From Portsmouth the regiment marched direct to Birmingham, being cheered in every village and town on the way. In recognition of their services in the Crimea all ranks received a medal and clasp for Sebastopol and also the Turkish medal. The word 'Sebastopol' was added to the regimental battle honours.

Lt.-Colonel Wilkie had by this time succeeded Colonel Parlby in command of the regiment which was now reduced to six troops. New dress regulations published in 1855 were also introduced for the first time. The hussar jacket with pelisse and gold and crimson sash was abolished and a tunic with skirt introduced. Strapped overalls were worn for mounted duty and officers distinguished by more or less braid on the collars and sleeves.

There followed a further reduction in strength and by this time the regiment had lost several officers and 300 fine men, discharged or transferred to other regiments. A few months later the outbreak of the Indian Mutiny caused the government to order a return to eight troops. This involved enlisting 407 recruits during the next two years, with the consequent problems of training, but by the time the regiment moved to Aldershot in 1858 it was once again efficient in drill and discipline. When Lt.-Colonel Valentine Baker succeeded Colonel Wilkie in command at Hounslow in 1860 it was in first rate order.

Having been senior major for some years, Lt.-Colonel Baker had already made his mark on the regiment, but for the next thirteen years under his command the Tenth rose to new heights. One who served under him wrote later:

The 10th Hussars under Colonel Valentine Baker.

'As a commanding officer and military instructor he was able to invest the dry details of drill with the highest interest. He had the power of expressing himself most forcibly, simply, and distinctly, either in speaking or writing and no-one could ever be in his company without being impressed with the clearness and vigour of his mind.' At this time the army was at a transitional stage, in the process of adopting more modern methods of training and organization. While maintaining its old reputation for smartness in drill and appearance, the Tenth under Valentine Baker led the cavalry in more modern tactics and organization. It was the start of a new era.

The new Colonel was not slow in introducing and encouraging innovations. In July 1860 two squadrons, one saddled and one unsaddled, practised travelling by train between Islington and Holloway to test the practicability of this means of transport for troops. Nor were any opportunities for sport missed. Regimental steeplechases were at once introduced and became an annual, eagerly competed event, the Colonel presenting the 'Baker Cup' for the winner. At Norwich that winter every advantage was taken of the good shooting available and when stationed in York the following year the officers were encouraged to hunt regularly, thus making many lasting friendships with the sporting people of Yorkshire. The popularity of the Tenth in York was also probably enhanced by the efforts of a troop stationed there in extinguishing a fire that had started in the city. In any event everyone was pleased to find them stationed there a further year.

In 1863 Earl Beauchamp was transferred to the Colonelcy of the 2nd Life Guards. In his place His Royal Highness Albert Edward, Prince of Wales, was gazetted Colonel. Once again the Tenth had a Prince of Wales as its Colonel and, according to an earlier history, 'it was largely due to his encouragement and support that Colonel Valentine Baker's career with the regiment proved such a successful one'.

The same year found the regiment posted to Ireland again, passing the winter in Dublin. At the same time Colonel Baker, who had been over in Austria observing their system of non-pivot drill, which was much discussed in military circles, received permission to try this method with the regiment. The Tenth were soon convinced that it was far and away simpler, reducing the number of movements required and far faster in execution.

During the winter of 1864, while Private Douglas was busy writing his book in the barracks at Cahir, the officers were enjoying a good season's hunting with their own pack, the Rock Harriers, hunted by Captain Molyneux, with Lord Valentia and Private Bowkett as whips. These country quarters were enjoyed by all, but meanwhile the Fenians were growing in strength preparatory to their attempt to overthrow the government and set up a republic in Ireland.

In May 1865 the Prince of Wales visited Dublin to open the International Exhibition. The Tenth formed his escort and were later reviewed along with the troops of the garrison in Phoenix Park. With the end of the Civil War in America the same year, many Irish Americans returned to Ireland, armed and looking for a fight. These swelled the Fenian ranks, forming themselves into cells, or circles, presided over by a centre. During that summer this led to much civil disturbance and the troops were kept constantly on the alert, but no doubt the Tenth enjoyed some good hunting in the winter months.

It was in the following year that Colonel Baker introduced the Regimental Call, taken from the opening movement of 'The Song of the Huguenot Soldiers', from the opera 'The Huguenots'. The custom of the band playing two hymns every evening between the first and second post, followed by 'God Save the Queen' was also instituted at this time. In similar ways Colonel Valentine Baker constantly encouraged the growth of the regimental pride and spirit.

A certain Jock Devoy, a Fenian agent who had the task of introducing circles into the British Army, admitted: 'I succeeded very well with all the regiments of the Dublin Garrison, except the 10th Hussars. They were picked men, at least physically. Morally and mentally they were also above the average, which was not high, of the army.'

Fortunately for him, there already was a Fenian agent in the Tenth, who had enlisted in England in 1863, especially for the purpose. His name was John Boyle O'Reilly and in other circumstances he would almost certainly have gone far in the regiment, for he was extremely intelligent, well educated and popular with all ranks. It is also to his credit that he was not a particularly good conspirator. According to a biographer: 'A handsome, lithely built, young fellow of twenty, O'Reilly was the model soldier . . . with boyish recklessness he embroidered rebel devices on the underside of his saddle cloth and the lining of his military greatcoat'.

Inevitably he was caught. Charged with 'knowledge of an intended mutiny', he was tried by court-martial on the eve of his twenty-second birthday in 1866 and formally sentenced to death, although Colonel Baker testified in his defence that he was always a good soldier. The sentence was commuted to life imprisonment and subsequently to twenty years' transportation to Western Australia. Some years later he escaped to America, married a girl of Irish descent, and became a respected newspaper editor.

The Fenian troubles came to a head in 1867 with the outbreak known as the 'Phoenix Conspiracy', when the intention was to take over the barracks and start an armed revolution throughout the country. The government however was fully informed of the details and the whole affair proved a fiasco. A flying column of fifty mounted and fifty dismounted men was led by Colonel Baker and proved instrumental in dealing with the conspirators in the south.

The Tenth once again proved themselves excellent fire-fighters, putting out a fire at the Haig distillery in Dundalk

A 10th Hussar officer (with striped trousers) enjoying a bit of fun off duty whilst on an officers' training course at Hythe.

in February, for which they were thanked by the resident magistrate. Subsequently, in June, they put out another fire in Dundalk, for which they were duly thanked by the mayor. Thereafter life seems to have been more peaceful and less eventful.

After H.R.H. the Prince of Wales had paid another visit to Dublin in 1868, escorted by the regiment, the Tenth returned to Aldershot. At this time the non-pivot drill was the subject of great discussion and the Tenth were much visited, officially and unofficially to see it practised. Although several other regiments received permission to adopt it and all approved, it was eventually rejected. The familiar pivot system was re-introduced, only to be abolished in due course and the non-pivot system eventually adopted by the British Army.

It was through Colonel Baker's strong representations that in 1869 cavalry regiments were formed into four squadrons instead of eight troops, both for administrative and tactical purposes. This was opposed throughout the service by junior captains reluctant to give up command of their troops, imagining that the value of the commission they had purchased might thus be depreciated. In this, as in many other ways, the purchase system had hindered changes in the army and it was a great step forward when it was abolished two years later.

The first of a series of large scale manoeuvres and field days was introduced this year. The cavalry at Aldershot was divided into two brigades, one consisting of the Tenth and Inniskillings under Colonel Baker. The use of flags for signalling purposes was first tried out on this occasion. The Tenth also adopted the use of flags with the regimental colours in front of each tent when in camp.

While under canvas at Aldershot that year Captain 'Chicken' Hartopp read an article in *The Field* about 'hockey on horseback' in India and suggested trying it out. In a short while several of the officers were trying to hit a billiard ball about with walking sticks from horseback. The idea appealed to them and they ordered ponies from Ireland and set about improving the sticks and ball. From this emerged the modern game of polo.

Later in 1869 the regiment returned to Brighton for the first time since 1829. While there the following year the depot troop of the 11th Hussars was attached to them during the temporary closure of the Cavalry Depot at Canterbury. From there and Hounslow in 1870 and 1871 the Tenth were twice inspected by the Queen while the Prince of Wales marched at their head. They also provided escorts for the Queen (a function thereafter only performed by the Life Guards) and the Queen's Guard at the opening of the Albert Hall. A further inspection by the Crown Prince of Prussia followed. It was all reminiscent of the old days under the Prince Regent, but there was now the difference that the Tenth were professional soldiers of the highest order beneath their smart appearance, as they proved in subsequent large-scale manoeuvres.

It was not however all parades and manoeuvres. During the regimental races in 1871 they also introduced a Hunt race in which the riders rode from point to point. Although they had previously held a similar race in Ireland it was then a complete novelty in England. Shortly afterwards they held their first inter-regimental polo game and a condensed report read as follows:

'Hockey on Horseback
'Nearly all fashionable London journeyed from town to Hounslow on Tuesday to witness a new game called "Hockey on Horseback" between the Officers of the 10th Prince of Wales's Hussars (sic) and Officers of the 9th Queen's Royal Lancers, who had come from Aldershot.

'The game took place on Hounslow Heath and the various equipages quite surrounded the ground allotted to the players. Posts some twenty yards apart marked the goals. The distance between them a little under 200 yards. The sticks used were like those used in hockey. Both sides wore mob caps with different coloured tassels attached. The ball, a little sphere of white bone, was thrown up by a sergeant major of the 10th, who then galloped off the ground. The eight players on each side, who had taken up position in front of their goals, then galloped for the ball at the best speed of their active, wiry little $12\frac{1}{2}$ hands high ponies. The game lasted for an hour and a half, with ten minutes interval. The Hussars gained three goals to the Lancers two. Though general remarks make it evident the new game is one most fitted for cavalry soldiers it was more remarkable for the language used by the players than anything else.'

In November of 1871 the Prince of Wales was dangerously ill with typhoid. On his recovery there was a ceremonial thanksgiving service in February 1872 attended by the Queen and royal family, at which the Tenth formed part of the procession. At the ensuing regimental dinner in June, the Prince of Wales presented the officers with a bronze statuette of himself in his uniform as Colonel of the 10th Hussars.

Several brigade exercises and sham fights took place in 1872. In the first the 7th and 10th Hussars were brigaded with the 12th Lancers under Colonel Valentine Baker. In a later, much larger, affair in Wiltshire, involving 30,000 troops and lasting a fortnight the value of his policy in only buying blood horses for the regiment rather than larger horses was fully vindicated. They lasted infinitely better and were instrumental in victory for their side being achieved by the actions of the Tenth.

Shortly after these last manoeuvres in September the regiment learned that it was being posted to India once again. They sailed in January 1873 in the troopship *Jumna*. After thirteen years Colonel Valentine Baker relinquished the command to Lt.-Colonel C. C. Molyneux and went on half pay. The regiment owed him a great deal. One who served under him wrote later: 'Valentine Baker had all the tastes and qualifications which peculiarly fit a man to distinguish himself as a soldier and to impress his influence on others. . . . Generous, brave and kind-hearted, he left a reputation in the 10th Hussars, which will not soon be forgotten.'

Chapter
5

THE Tenth were stationed initially at Muttra, near
Agra, which proved a very popular and healthy
station. The officers were soon enjoying pig-sticking
and polo, more like the modern version than their 'hockey
on horseback'. The N.C.O.s also played polo and both
N.C.O.s and men were able to obtain good sport shooting
close at hand, supplementing their rations with welcome
extras. A pack of hounds brought over from England provided good sport hunting jackal in the winter months. In
addition to cricket, boxing and fives, a regimental theatre
was started and open air concerts were held regularly,
which proved considerable attractions, with the bandsmen
of the Tenth, as ever, providing a competent pool of
talent.

It is doubtful if Private Douglas would have recognised
the scene, for even in matters of drill and military training
the Tenth had learned to avoid monotony. A couple of
brass six-pounder guns were used to teach gun drill under
tuition from the R.A. Troop horses were trained to work
with the guns and as a result an efficient artillery section
was brought into being. The hard exercise involved was
found good for the health of all concerned and the regiment
was commended for the innovation by the inspecting
general.

A change of dress was made in 1875 with the abolition of
strapped overalls and the introduction of pantaloons and
jack boots. Colonel Molyneux also replaced the old cloth
stable jackets with blue serge jackets for general use. These
were subsequently used regularly on the march and during
the winter months and became the eventual army pattern.

In 1875 also the Tenth received astonishing news of an old Tenth Hussar in England. This concerned none other than their late, greatly admired, commanding officer, Colonel Valentine Baker. After relinquishing command of the regiment, he had spent a year on half pay in the near east, the fruits of which subsequently appeared in a book entitled *Clouds in the East*, in which he clearly outlined the coming troubles between Russia and Turkey. He had then returned to take up a staff job at Aldershot, where the Duke of Cambridge had publicly referred to him as one of the best officers in the army and a brilliant career seemed certain to lie ahead. Thus it must have been astounding to learn that he was to appear in court on a treble charge of assault with intent to ravage, indecent assault and common assault.

The facts were simply these. Colonel Baker entered a train at Liphook for Waterloo on the hot afternoon of June 17. There were no corridors in those days and the only other occupant of the carriage was a Miss Dickinson, aged twenty-two, sister to a barrister and an army officer, of eminent respectability. Shortly afterwards, as they were travelling at forty miles an hour, the train driver looked back and saw a female clinging to an open carriage door. He stopped the train. Miss Dickinson, in a highly emotional state, accused the Colonel of attacking her. She was removed to a carriage with a clergyman and the train continued to Waterloo, where enquiries were made. Colonel Baker, expostulating that the girl had simply misunderstood him, gave his name and address. Shortly afterwards the case was committed for trial.

Every single circumstance seems to have conspired against him receiving a fair trial. Only the previous year there had been a particularly bad case involving an army officer and a girl in a railway carriage. It was a hot June and July and the Press could find little else of interest to fill their columns. If ever a man was crucified and pre-judged by the Press and public opinion before his trial it was Colonel Valentine Baker, but that was the least of it.

Of all days, the trial took place on August Bank Holiday Monday at Croydon and so great was the public interest that the court was besieged. Such a vast crowd assembled outside that it was frequently hard to hear the proceedings. Worse still, Mr. Justice Brett, the judge, was known to be particularly severe, especially in sexual offences, and from the start it was obvious that he was hostile to Colonel Baker. Furthermore, in those days of rigid class distinctions, the jury, composed mostly of small Croydon shopkeepers, were hardly the Colonel's peers, able to comprehend his notions of honour and attitudes of mind. On those and other counts it was obvious that Colonel Baker's counsel confidently anticipated an adjournment to a more suitable occasion when a fair trial could be expected, but Mr. Justice Brett refused to countenance the suggestion and the trial went ahead in these almost farcical conditions.

In effect it was a straight issue as to whether Miss Dickinson or the Colonel was lying. Each gave a similar account of a very innocuous opening conversation concerning the weather and the merits of the countryside. Thereafter Miss Dickinson depicted the Colonel with glaring eyes making amorous advances and putting his arm round her waist. This so terrified her that, after pulling the communication cord, which failed to work, she opened the door and stepped onto the running board outside. The Colonel's version was simply that she appeared to have misunderstood some remark he made and took fright, after which he tried to coax her back into the carriage.

No court today would have accepted such unsupported evidence. With modern psychiatric knowledge every court, policeman and probation officer is familiar with the common wish-fulfilment fancies of young females, the hysterical self-delusions which often lead to a genuine belief that they have been attacked and nearly raped. This was a classic case. It was a hot June day and the Colonel was a powerfully built man with a fiercesome black walrus moustache and piercing dark eyes, just the sort of figure to give rise to such a fantasy in the mind of an impressionable young female wilting in the heat. Nor could the Colonel, expert at handling men, be expected to cope with a hysterical female in such circumstances. Few men could.

In Regency days, or today, the case would never have arisen, but this was the height of the Victorian era and a very different matter. There was no concrete evidence on which one would have hung a dog, but in the circumstances the Colonel did not stand a dog's chance. He was found guilty on the lesser two counts, condemned to a year in prison and fined £500. He was automatically disgraced and cashiered, but his wife, daughter and friends, of whom he had many, all stood by him. Nor was there a man of the 10th Hussars who believed him guilty, for those who knew him well were aware that it was completely outside his character.

Meanwhile in India Colonel Baker's training continued to bear fruit and the Tenth continued to remain in the forefront. A new system of working by dismounted sections was pioneered by Major Lord Ralph Kerr for advanced cavalry work, the aim being to bring as strong a body of men to a given point as quickly as possible. Three men out of each section dismounted at a chosen point and their horses were galloped to the nearest cover by another, who brought them back when required. The practice was soon introduced to the service.

In 1876 the regiment acted as escorts and guard of honour on the arrival of the Prince of Wales in Delhi and throughout his subsequent month's tour. Shortly afterwards Colonel Molyneux retired from the army and was succeeded in command of the regiment by Lt.-Colonel Lord Ralph Kerr. Under him the Tenth returned to Muttra, where the familiar routine was taken up once more.

58

The following year Queen Victoria was proclaimed Empress of India at an Imperial Assembly in Delhi, attended by the Tenth. A salute of 101 guns, which caused a stampede of the native Prince's ceremonial elephants, was followed by a grand march past of the troops when the Viceroy, Lord Lytton, took the salute. In commemoration of the event the Tenth received a silver trumpet with banderol and sling. Soon afterwards the regiment received orders to move from Muttra to relieve the 4th Hussars at Rawalpindi, which entailed a long cross country march into the Punjab, where they arrived early in 1878.

Army Museums Ogilby Trust

A group of officers from several regiments, members of Lord Roberts' expedition to Afghanistan—a 10th Hussar is seated in the centre.

In late November 1878 hostilities broke out with Afghanistan and a squadron of the 10th Hussars were the first troops to enter the country at the head of a column under General Roberts, later Lord Roberts. In January 1879, when the British camp at Matun was surrounded by about 1,500 hostile Afghans the squadron of the Tenth, accompanied by a squadron of the 5th Punjab Cavalry, under command of Colonel Hugh Gough, V.C., drove them back into the hills. Later they covered the rearguard, when the British withdrew, and repelled a force of about 5,000 tribesmen who swarmed down onto the plain. On their return to the regimental headquarters at Jellalabad, Lord Roberts expressed his 'deep regret at losing so fine a body of men from his command.' He added: 'No soldiers could have behaved more steadily in quarters or done better service in the field'.

Meanwhile the main body of the regiment had joined the cavalry brigade of the First Division of the Peshawar Valley Field Force, made up of the 10th Hussars, the Guide's Cavalry and the 11th Bengal Lancers under Brigadier C. Gough, V.C. In November 1878 they advanced up the Khyber Pass to storm the fort at Ali Musjid. After a day's sharp action the fort was abandoned during the night by the Afghan troops and the cavalry brigade then marched on Jellalabad on the banks of the Kabul river, which they found had been evacuated. There they encamped and set up their headquarters, engaging in several minor scouting expeditions.

On the night of March 31, as part of a combined attack, a squadron of the 10th Hussars and a squadron of the 11th Bengal Lancers under Major E. A. Wood of the Tenth were ordered to cross the Kabul river and take up a position in the rear of the tribes on the far side by dawn. The Kabul ford was a treacherous one in the shape of an irregular S bend. The squadron of the 11th Bengal Lancers went first with an Afghan guide. In almost pitch darkness the squadron of the Tenth followed closely on the tails of their two rear baggage mules.

As each file of the Bengal Lancers crossed they must have been imperceptibly edged downstream by the current. Finally the two mules were swept off their feet. Before they realised what had happened the entire squadron of the Tenth behind them were also swept downstream. Weighed down by their heavy marching equipment they had little or no chance in the swift current and swollen icy waters.

Captain Spottiswoode in the front was only saved by the efforts of his particularly powerful charger. Lt. Greenwood and Lt. Grenfell, both almost exhausted, managed to rescue Private Goddard between them and staggered ashore with him. Private Cowley, who had swum with his horse until it drowned, managed to get ashore with difficulty and returned to the assistance of Lt. the Hon. J. Napier.

Five others, who had managed to get rid of their belts and arms, also managed to reach the shore. The remainder, one officer and forty-six N.C.O.s and men, were drowned, their bodies being swept miles downstream. Those remaining in camp, alarmed by the return of wet and riderless horses went to the ford to help, but arrived too late. Major E. A. Wood, unaware of the full scale of the tragedy, went on with the remainder of his force to the agreed position, but the enemy had escaped into the mountain.

On the same night the remaining two squadrons of the Tenth marched with a force under Brigadier Charles Gough, V.C., to operate on the south side of the Kabul river. About 1 p.m. the next day a large body of the enemy was found holding a plateau. General Gough advanced with the artillery and cavalry and then withdrew, to entice the tribesmen onto the plain towards the infantry. The strategy was successful and, as the infantry attacked, the Tenth and the Guides charged on the flank killing upwards of 400 and pursuing them some miles. This cavalry action at Futtehabad was the most decisive of the Frontier War. The Tenth's casualties were seven men wounded.

When they returned to camp the full tragedy of the Kabul disaster was realised. The Prince of Wales sent a telegram to Colonel Lord Ralph Kerr: 'Express condolence and sympathy with regiment at disaster crossing Kabul river.' Kipling was moved to immortalise it in verse:

> 'The river's up an' brimmin',
> An' there's arf a Squadron swimmin'
> Cross the Ford o' Kabul River, in the dark
> You can 'ear the 'orses threshin',
> You can 'ear the men a splashin',
> Cross the Ford o' Kabul River, in the dark
> There's the river loud an' fallin',
> But it ain't no use o' callin',
> Cross the Ford o' Kabul River, in the dark.'

This was not the end of the regiment's misfortunes. After the Afghans had submitted in May, the Tenth was marching down the Khyber Pass in June, the hottest month of the year, when a wave of virulent cholera hit them. Before they had reached Ali Musjid in what became aptly known as 'The Death March' thirty-eight men had died in thirty-eight hours and the features after death were so distorted that it was often impossible to recognise the individual. In this way mistakes occurred and for some days it was not possible to make a correct roll of the casualties. In addition a further sixteen men died of other diseases during this campaign, so that by the time the regiment had returned to Rawalpindi their numbers were greatly depleted.

In his report on the campaign Lt.-General Sir Sam Browne wrote of:

> 'the high reputation which the conscientious performance of their duties by every man of that fine Regiment the 10th Prince of Wales's Own Royal Hussars, has

earned for it. The Regiment is one that any service in the world would be proud of. Tried in the field at Futtehabad against greatly superior numbers, tested in many and long day's reconnaissance and outpost duty, in the accident at the ford of the Kabul River, and in the attack of cholera while passing through the Khyber, the high discipline and soldierlike qualities of this noble Regiment have ever shone forth, proving no less the efficiency of the present officers than the careful training it has received in the past.'

A medal with the clasp 'Ali Musjid' was granted to all those who took part in the campaign. In commemoration of it the Tenth were permitted to bear the words 'Ali Musjid,' and 'Afghanistan 1878–1879' on their appointments. A memorial window to those lost of all ranks was placed in the All Saints Church, Aldershot.

In August 1879 the newly signed peace treaty was violated by the massacre of the English residency at Kabul, starting the second phase of the Afghan War. Due to their heavy losses in the first phase as well as to a persistent outbreak of dengue fever the Tenth were kept at Rawalpindi. So much sickness continued throughout the summer of 1880 that they were ordered to change their quarters to Lucknow, which was a healthy, well situated station. Here they settled down to the familiar routine of polo, pig-sticking, theatres and concerts, gradually regaining their health and efficiency during 1881.

Lt.-Colonel A. E. Wood succeeded Colonel Lord Ralph Kerr in command of the regiment in 1881 and in 1882 khaki replaced the old white drill, but otherwise the routine of the station continued normally. With the passing of another year the Tenth had completed an eleven year tour of duty and in 1884 came the welcome news that they were to return home.

The regiment embarked for England in February 1884. To their pleasure they found themselves again on the troopship *Jumna*, in which they had sailed out from England eleven years previously. Accompanied by their wives and children they settled down to the long journey home once more via the Suez Canal.

We must now return again to Colonel Valentine Baker. After serving his prison sentence with characteristic courage, he found his wife and daughter and many friends ready to welcome him, but understandably he did not stay in England long. In 1877 the war he had foreseen broke out between Russia and Turkey and he was offered the post of Major-General in the Turkish Army, where he performed many magnificent feats of arms, earning the title of 'Pasha', the equivalent of Baron. Some idea of his fighting qualities is obtained from this extract from the report of a war correspondent present at the battle of Takhessan:

'Eight squadrons of Turkish regular cavalry came out from behind a low hill on the Turkish right. They were led by a man on a fine grey Arab, the grandest horseman I have every seen. They came round the hill at a trot, then broke into a gallop and came swooping down on the left flank of the Russians, tearing through them like an express train through a flock of sheep.

'I could not help watching the man on the grey Arab and I saw his sabre go sweeping up and down and all round, like lightning flashes. He made a lane through the ranks of the Russian Infantry in whatever direction he went. Some bodies of the Russian cavalry came out to meet him and they came into contact in a large field of high maize.

'But there was no holding back Baker and his Turks and the Russian Cavalry was soon tearing back as hard as they could go, to get under the shelter of their guns. The Turkish Cavalry followed them hard, like tigers who had once tasted blood and longed for more. I saw a shell explode within a few yards of the Pasha; his horse fell and down he came. That was the end of the grey Arab, but not of his master, for Baker was up in a moment, on the charger of a common trooper, in the middle of his men, hacking like a very Hercules.

The old Artillery Officer, who was standing quite close to me, laid down his field glasses and said:

'I swear by the Prophet that the Infidel who commands our Cavalry fights with the courage of ten thousand tigers.'
'And yet,'

said a younger Artillery Officer:

'Allah has smitten the English with such mad blindness that they allowed a man like him to leave their Army.'

In 1882 General Baker was offered the position of Commander-in-Chief of the Egyptian Army. He resigned his Turkish commission to accept it, but the British Government then in control refused to confirm the offer and instead gave him command of the Egyptian Gendarmerie, a semi-military mixed force. In 1884 he was sent with these and a hastily conscripted army to quell the Sudanese rebels at Suakim. Only his high sense of duty made him attempt this hopeless task with what amounted to little more than a rabble. It was indeed only due to his consummate leadership that he extricated them without complete annihilation after they had been decisively defeated.

In order to retrieve this reverse the Tenth, while sailing up the Red Sea, were diverted to Suakim and ordered to prepare for action. Thus, by a fantastic freak of fate, they were reunited with their old Colonel. He was enthusiastically received on board *Jumna* with a guard of honour, the whole regiment turning out to cheer him, while the band played 'Auld Lang Syne'. He then explained that he was offering the horses of his Gendarmerie to the 10th Hussars.

The Royal Navy cheerfully lent sailmakers and others to help make nose bags, head ropes, water bottles and other items of kit in which the regiment was deficient. Everything about the campaign was a makeshift. Water supplies were inadequate, rations poor, and the promised camping equipment almost non-existent, the men sleeping in the open throughout the campaign, without even blankets for cover. However the Tenth were soon re-embarked for Trinkitat, four hours south from Suakim, where they joined the force under General Graham detailed to relieve a beleaguered Egyptian garrison at Tokar. This force consisted of the 10th and 19th Hussars, two brigades of infantry and the Naval brigade, with whom the Tenth had already established very friendly relations.

On the morning of February 29 the march began to El Teb, where the enemy were encamped. The infantry marched in a large square, covered by a squadron of the 10th Hussars with the remainder of the cavalry brigade on the left flank. The enemy were discovered on some sand hills round the wells at El Teb. Following familiar tactics the cavalry advanced to draw their fire and then retreated. The Soudanese, after firing their Krupps guns at the infantry square, tried to rush it, but failed to get within 150 yards. The cavalry then advanced and, finding large numbers of the enemy in the bush, charged repeatedly, finally dispersing them.

During the action Bandsman Hayes of the Tenth, a notable boxer, distinguished himself by dismounting and attacking a group of Arabs near a fallen comrade with his fists, knocking them down and then remounting, for which he was subsequently awarded a medal at Windsor. Before the regiment had bivouacked, General Baker, with a bullet from a Krupp's gun still in his cheek, rode round to the lines of the Tenth to congratulate them and enquire about their losses. These were two officers, one N.C.O. and three men killed and five men wounded.

One officer of the Tenth was greatly disappointed to miss the battle. The Adjutant, Captain the Earl of Airlie, who had gone home early on leave, was in Paris when his sister

The charge of the 10th Hussars at El Teb.

wired him of the diversion to Suakim and impending action. The only means of getting there was by chartering a steamship, which he promptly did. The sole passenger on board a Wilson liner, he spent most of his time in the engine room urging them to greater speed. In spite of all his efforts they arrived on March 2, two days too late, by which time the regiment had returned to Suakim.

He was heard bemoaning his luck at 'missing the fun'.

'Never mind,' Major Gough replied. 'You'll soon be in the thick of it. Besides it's not much fun for any of us. I haven't had these jack boots off for eleven days now.'

Another action soon followed on March 13 against the Arab stronghold of Tamai, where 10,000 were encamped. The infantry advanced in two squares with the cavalry in reserve in the rear. An order to charge was misheard and a gap formed in a square, through which the Arabs charged, causing it to fall back some distance. The cavalry was then ordered to charge, but, as the enemy was behind a cliff in a deep nullah, they were forced to halt. A dismounted volley and enfilade fire held the Arabs back until the main force came up and brought such heavy fire to bear that the enemy were soon in full retreat. Soon afterwards Tamai was taken, the Tenth's only casualties being one N.C.O. and one private wounded.

There was no further heavy fighting, but the regiment was engaged in reconnaissance and convoy work until March 29, when it was decided that the emergency was over. The Tenth then finally re-embarked on *Jumna* once more, sailing up the Suez Canal and returning home on April 21, 1884.

In commemoration of the campaign the Tenth were permitted to bear the words 'Egypt 1884' on their appointments. On June 27, H.R.H. the Prince of Wales inspected the regiment and silver medals were presented to officers and men by the Princess of Wales. The Prince concluded a congratulatory speech to the regiment: 'It is now twenty-

68

one years since Her Majesty conferred upon me the honour of Colonel of the 10th Hussars and I feel proud to be connected with it.'

Amongst the old officers of the regiment present on this occasion was General Valentine Baker and it is interesting to note he was thus rehabilitated before his death three years later in 1887. The following verses by Mr. Clement Scott, which appeared in *Punch* of March 15, 1884, and which were widely reprinted throughout almost every paper in the country due to their very opportune reference to him, may well have had their effect.

A Tale of the Tenth Hussars

When the sand of the lonely desert has covered the plains
of strife,
Where the English fought for the rescue and the Arab
stood for his life:

Army Museums Ogilby Trust

10th Hussars: a detachment of the Light Camel Corps as volunteers for the Nile Expedition. Shorncliffe Barracks 1884.

When the crash of the battle is over and healed are our
  wounds and scars,
There will live in our island story a Tale of the Tenth
  Hussars.
They had charged in the grand old fashion with furious
  shout and swoop,
With a 'Follow me, Lads!' from the Colonel and an
  answering roar from the troop;
From the Staff, as the troopers past it, in glory of pride
  and pluck,
They heard, and they never forgot it one following
  shout 'Good Luck!'
Wounded and worn he sat there, in silence of pride and
  pain,
The man who had led them often, but was never to lead
  again.
Think of the secret anguish! Think of the dull remorse!
To see the Hussars sweep past him, unled by the old
  White Horse!
An alien, not a stranger; with the heart of a comrade still,
He had borne his sorrow bravely, as a soldier must and
  will;
And when the battle was over, in deepening gloom and
  shade,
He followed the Staff in silence, and rode to the Grand
  Parade;
For the Tenth had another hero, all ripe for the General's
  praise,
Who was called to the front that evening, by the name
  of Trooper Hayes;
He had slashed his way to fortune, when scattered,
  unhorsed, alone,
And in saving the life of a comrade had managed to
  guard his own.
The General spoke out bravely, as ever a soldier can—
'The Army's proud of your valour; the Regiment's
  proud of their man!'
Then across that lonely desert, at the close of the
  General's praise,

Came a cheer, then a quick short tremble, on the lips of
   Trooper Hayes.
'Speak out,' said the kindly Colonel, 'if you've anything,
   Lad, to say;
'Your Queen and your dear old country shall hear what
   you've done today!'
But the Trooper gnawed his chin-strap, then sheepishly
   hung his head;
'Speak out, old chap!' said his comrades. With an effort
   at last he said—
'I came to the front with my pals here, the boys and the
   brave old tars,
'I've fought for my Queen and country and rode with
   the Tenth Hussars;
'I'm proud of the fine old regiment!'—then the Colonel
   shook his hand—
'So I'll ask one single favour from my Queen and my
   native land!
'There sits by your side on the Staff, sir, a man we are
   proud to own!
'He was struck down first in the battle, but never was
   heard to groan;
'If I've done ought to deserve it,'—then the Colonel
   smiled 'Of course!'
'Give back to the Tenth their Colonel—the Man on the
   old White Horse!
'If ever a man bore up, sir, as a soldier should with pluck,
'And fought with a savage sorrow the demon of cursed
   ill-luck—
'That man he sits before you! Give us back with his
   wounds and scars,
'The man who has sorely suffered, and is loved by the
   Tenth Hussars!'
Then a cheer went up from his comrades, and echoed
   across the sand,
And was borne on the wings of mercy to the heart of his
   native land,
Where the Queen on her throne will hear it, and the
   Colonel Prince will praise

The words of a simple soldier just uttered by Trooper
 Hayes.
Let the moralist stoop to mercy, that balm of all souls
 that live;
For better than all forgetting, is the wonderful word
 'Forgive!'

Chapter

6

IN the Autumn of 1884, after they had settled down at
Shorncliffe, the Tenth provided a contingent of two
officers and forty-five other ranks to join the Light
Camel Corps in the Nile Expeditionary under Lord
Wolseley. They were under the command of Lt.-Colonel
Brabazon and Lord Airlie served as Brigade Major, being
severely wounded. They returned in July 1885 to find the
regiment about to move to Aldershot, where in 1886
H.R.H. Prince Albert Victor, Duke of Clarence, eldest son
of the Prince of Wales, joined the regiment as a subaltern.

In the same year Colonel A. E. Wood, the sixth member
of his family to serve in the Tenth since Waterloo, was succeeded in command by Lt.-Colonel R. S. Liddell. In the
spring a point-to-point steeplechase took place between
five subalterns of the Tenth and five subalterns of their old
friends and rivals the Blues, a cup being presented by the
Prince of Wales. The Tenth won with two out of three in
at the finish, first and third.

Soon afterwards the Tenth received permission to stage
a 'cavalry raid.' In effect this was a three day tactical exercise under active service conditions, a revolutionary idea in
those days. The progress of the exercise was followed with
considerable interest and the idea quickly became accepted
practice. At about the same time the regiment tried out a
new type of smaller and lighter busby. This also met with
immediate approval and promptly became the accepted
pattern for Hussars and Horse Artillery.

These were not the only innovations Colonel Liddell
introduced, although due to the retiral system then in force
he was only in command of the regiment for eighteen

months. At his own expense he bought a Nordenfeldt machine gun, which he then equipped with a two wheeled galloping carriage, suitable for harnessing to a horse. This soon proved so useful that six more were purchased and with some modifications were issued to other regiments.

In 1887 the Tenth took part in the celebrations for Queen Victoria's Jubilee. In a subsequent parade they were inspected by Prince William of Prussia, afterwards Emperor of Germany. They also took part in a Jubilee Review before the Queen, in which about 40,000 troops of all arms were present. The Prince of Wales marched past at the head of the regiment, with Prince Albert Victor leading the right-hand troop of the leading squadron.

After his short but significant period of command Colonel Liddell perpetuated his connection with the Tenth by producing a beautifully illustrated 566 page history of the regiment. He was succeeded in 1887 by Lt.-Colonel Viscount Downe, who had joined the 2nd Life Guards as a cornet in 1865 and served with them until 1886. By succeeding to the command of the Tenth he increased the rivalry and friendship between the two regiments, who each now referred to the other as their '2nd battalion'. In the same year the Tenth was remarkably lucky on the turf. Lt. Baird's horse Playfair won the Grand National and at the Grand Military Meeting at Sandown Park practically every winner was either ridden or owned by a 10th Hussar.

In those halcyon days the standard of officers and men had never been higher. The Tenth was full of notable characters. Particularly outstanding was the adjutant, Captain the Hon. Julian Byng, later Viscount Byng of Vimy, but more generally known as 'Bungo'. It was due largely to his efforts that while posted close to the temptations of London the defaulters sheet was invariably clean. His efforts to provide sport and canteen facilities for the men, including his versifying efforts, were long remembered. To him was attributed the popular canteen chorus:

'Ours is a happy, happy home,
From the dear old Tenth I never want to roam,
What with drill and sports and cricket,
For my "twenty-one" I'll stick it,
Ours is a happy, happy home.'

In 1888 the regiment moved to York. It was twenty-five years since they had last been stationed there but they were soon welcomed back. The regimental cricket team at this time included one Oxford and one Cambridge Blue, the captain and two members of the Eton eleven and a member of the Harrow eleven, as well as other excellent players. In their first year they never lost a match.

Colonel Downe was far ahead of contemporary military thought in such matters as allowing N.C.O.s to wear flannels when off duty. He also encouraged rowing on the river Ouse so that the regiment soon produced some excellent fours. The Tenth also introduced football here and this soon became a very popular regimental sport. It is easy to understand why this period was long remembered in the regiment.

In 1889 the Prince of Wales stayed in the barracks for a week-end and took command of the regiment. In the regimental point-to-point held then, Prince Albert came in fourth. After an inspection and drill at Knavesmire the Prince of Wales personally led the regiment back to the barracks.

In 1890 a detachment of the Tenth were sent to North Wales to enforce the unpopular tithe collections. They arrived at Denbigh to assist the collector, Mr. Stevens, and were at first billeted in various hotels. They succeeded fairly well in the Llanefyrd district, quietening the crowds and distraining a stack of hay in the notoriously difficult 'Nant' district. Then they moved to Llanfairtelhairn and were under canvas in such bad weather that they were literally washed away. It is recorded that: 'the anti-Tithe party were highly delighted at the collapse of the camp and unmistakable signs of the wretched state of affairs that had prevailed'.

In 1891 the regiment returned to Ireland again. In January of 1892 Prince Albert Victor died at Sandringham while on leave. Colonel Viscount Downe and nine officers of the Tenth acted as pall bearers at his funeral and twenty N.C.O.s and men bore the coffin to the gun carriage and into St. George's Chapel. A message from the Prince and Princess of Wales read: "As long as they live they will ever remember with gratitude the never ceasing respect and devotion their son met with in the 10th Hussars, a gratitude which the poor young Duke also felt when serving in the regiment he was so proud of."

Shortly after the funeral Lord Downe was succeeded by Lt.-Colonel C. M. Wood, whose entire period of command was passed in Ireland. This proved an exceptionally peaceful period without any civil commotions and the Tenth seem to have enjoyed their posting almost as much as the period in York. In 1896 Lt.-Colonel Fisher-Childe succeeded Colonel C. M. Wood in command and in June 1897 the Tenth returned to Aldershot, where they were promptly engaged in the celebrations for Queen Victoria's Diamond Jubilee. With the exception of the Household troops they were probably the only regiment present at the Coronation of Queen Victoria and both Jubilees.

Another short period of home service at Aldershot and Canterbury ensued before the outbreak of the South African War in October 1899. On November 3 and 4 the regiment embarked from Liverpool for Capetown. 'A' Squadron and a troop of 'B' squadron with a battery of artillery were on board the *S.S. Ismore* and the rest of the regiment on *S.S. Colombia*, both cattle ships engaged on the Atlantic trade. They received a tremendous send-off from a crowd of nearly a hundred thousand people, but the weather at sea was bad and *Ismore* was delayed two days in the Mersey, having eventually to put back into Milford

'The Tenth don't dance.'

Haven because eighteen horses had died in the rough seas.

In order to make up time, the captain of the *Ismore* then disobeyed his instructions, which were to keep fifty miles off shore until he reached Capetown. Instead he laid his course direct to the port, thinking this would keep him twenty miles clear of Paternoster Point, fifty miles north of the Cape. This was not allowing for the two knot inshore current and at 2 a.m. on the morning of December 2 the *Ismore* struck the reef off Paternoster Point a mile from the shore and ripped her keel open, becoming a total wreck.

The behaviour of the troops was magnificent and there was no panic on board. The crew 'for the most part an evil and undesirable looking lot of foreigners' true to nautical tradition took to the rum casks and refused to take any further interest in the proceedings. Fortunately the sea was comparatively calm with only a heavy swell.

The troops all fell in at their allotted stations wearing life-jackets and under the directions of the ship's officers began to launch the boats, the first being launched without the bung in place so that it filled with water and the men had to be hurriedly withdrawn. It was about an hour and a half before the first was launched effectively, because in the meantime the Chief Engineer had drawn attention to the danger of water reaching the boilers and causing an explosion, so the tarpaulins had to be hastily cut from the covers for the horses on deck and used to prevent this possibility.

By 4 a.m. some Hottentots and a white man had come out from the shore in boats and by 8 a.m. most of the troops were safely on dry land. Major Alexander, the squadron leader, was the last to leave and soon afterwards the ship broke her back on the falling tide. Efforts to induce the horses to leave the ship had for the most part proved unavailing as they simply swam round the ship or headed for the open sea. Only seventeen were saved and the entire cargo of guns, ammunition and stores had to be abandoned.

After two days on the inhospitable shore the troops were ordered to march to St. Helena Bay fifteen miles away over thick sandy veldt in blazing sun in order to get to the nearest point where ships could pick them up. There they boarded the *Columbia*, from which the rest of the regiment had already disembarked. On December 6 the detachment finally landed at Capetown and were railed to Stellenbosch where they received Argentine remounts, tents, saddlery and arms. On the 19th they left for Arundel to rejoin the regiment, which had already been twice engaged with the Boers and lost one man killed and two wounded.

From this date until February 4 the Tenth were engaged

78

in operations under General French; a front of forty miles
had to be protected by a small cavalry force and the duties
were harassing, arduous and incessant. Many small engage-
ments were fought and casualties were frequent. On
January 4 Major C. B. Harvey was killed while gallantly
leading his squadron in a dismounted action.

On the 5th Sir John Milbanke was out with a patrol and
was shot in the pelvis. He had nearly returned to one of our
piquets when he saw that Corporal Barclay of his patrol had
had his horse shot and was under fire dismounted. He
promptly turned and galloped back, mounted the Corporal
on his horse and carried him back to the piquet where as
he dismounted he fainted from loss of blood. This act was
seen by General French and General Brabazon, who
recommended him for the Victoria Cross, which he even-

Hulton Picture Library

The South African War. Infantry and artillery fording the river Modder.

tually received from the Queen at one of the last public functions she attended.

On February 4 the regiment entrained at Rensburg and joined the army under Lord Roberts at Modder River, being brigaded with the Household Cavalry and the 12th Lancers under General Broadwood. They took part in the famous ride to the relief of Kimberley, when they had a four mile gallop under heavy cross fire at Klip Drift on the Reit River and occasional actions throughout the long march on short rations across burning veldt under a hot sun. Kimberley was relieved on February 15, but there was no rest for the cavalry, for at 1.30 a.m. on the morning of the 17th information was received that Cronje's army was retiring and that a large convoy was making for Koodooe's Ranch Drift.

The 2nd Cavalry Brigade with two batteries R.H.A. was ordered to try to cut them off and they marched at 3 a.m. After covering about twenty-five miles in darkness they arrived at a ridge overlooking the Modder River and saw the convoy trying to cross. Some shells from the R.H.A. soon stopped this attempt. Meanwhile a strong party of Boers started from the main force to reach a commanding kopje on the right flank and 'A' Squadron was ordered to take it first. A close race followed with the squadron capturing it in fine style, being shortly reinforced by 'B' Squadron. A picture of the incident now hangs in the Officer's Mess.

As a result of the Brigade's efforts the Boer Commandant Cronje, with some 5,000 Transvaal and Free State Burghers, stores, ammunition and transport, were forced to take refuge in the bends of the Modder River between Paardeburg and Wolveskraal Drifts. During the night of the 17th the infantry converged on Paardeburg and Cronje's position became hopeless. He was eventually forced to surrender on February 27 after much loss of life on both sides.

On March 6 the regiment as part of the Brigade moved to Osfontein, taking part in the battle at Poplar Drove on the 7th and at Driefontein on the 10th as part of the advance on Bloemfontein. The men were on half rations riding horses on quarter rations under semi-tropical sun in a land where water was scarce, yet on the night of the 12th in pitch darkness they reached Ferrara Spruit four miles from the capital of the Free State.

That night Sergeant Henry Engleheart was detached from the regiment to work with a squadron of mounted Pioneers whose task was to destroy the railway line beyond the town to prevent the escape of the enemy's rolling stock. This was done successfully with Sergeant Engleheart occupying a covering position close to a Boer piquet through which he had to cut his way back. Then under heavy shell and rifle fire he rescued Sapper Webb of the R.E.s who was dismounted in a deep spruit. For this gallant action he was awarded the Victoria Cross.

On March 13 President Steyn and his irreconcilables had fled from Bloemfontein and Lord Roberts took the surrender of the town. The regiment bivouacked for the first

Racing the Boers for the kopje above the Modder River.

time in months amid scenes of comparative civilisation. 'C' Squadron under Captain Kavanagh were encamped on a small farm called Noodhulp, owned by a Mr. and Mrs. Blockenhaager, who had fled for shelter from the British. There was good grazing, plenty of water and fat poultry and sheep around the farmhouse. Inevitably the squadron was soon eating freshly grilled mutton chops and chicken off Mrs. Blockenhaager's best china, when she returned in her wrath, a formidable and loquacious virago. Captain Kavanagh found her too much for him, but Colonel Fisher-Childe, with his well known charm, though persistently addressing her as Mrs. Huggermugger, sent her on her way rejoicing with 'chits' for all her commandeered property.

By this time the total available strength of the Tenth was under 180 but it had more horses fit for duty than the other

The 10th Hussars on field manoeuvres, circa *1897.*

two regiments in the Brigade and therefore on March 18 was ordered to form part of a column to go to Thaba N'Chu. This was on the road to Lady Brand in the centre of the richest grain growing belt of the Free State. On the 22nd, while the rest of the column remained in bivouac there, 'B' Squadron was detailed to reconnoitre towards Lady Brand, accompanied by some mounted infantry.

On March 29, leaving the Maxim gun and the mounted infantry on a hill above the town, the Squadron, barely thirty strong, entered Lady Brand and took the Landdrost prisoner. Almost at once 300 Boers were sighted converging from three sides at full gallop. Lord William Bentinck, the squadron leader, ordered the 'retire' and they galloped out of the town under heavy fire, retiring on the Maxim gun. The Landdrost was brought away as prisoner in his own Cape Cart, being encouraged to put on speed by Captain Chaplin with a revolver. Three men were wounded and four, including two of the wounded, taken prisoner.

With the enemy following in strength the squadron withdrew to rejoin the column at Thaba N'Chu in a forced march, covering between fifty and sixty miles in twenty-four hours. On March 30, about midday, as a Boer Commando was reported to be marching on Thaba N'Chu and another force was reported to be working round to cut off their retreat to the Modder River, the column was ordered to saddle up and the transport to move, with orders to cross the river and outspan on the far bank. The remainder of the column waited until dark and then withdrew, marching until 3 a.m., when they joined the transport across the river.

The site chosen for the bivouac was between the Modder River and the Koorn Spruit, or water course, running into it. By sheer bad luck it also happened that morning to be between the two Boer Commandos who had planned to attack the Modder River Water Works nearby. The force on the far side of the river had artillery and at 6 a.m. began shelling the British column while it was breakfasting.

Fortunately the shelling did little damage and the transport
and artillery, which could not return the fire, were sent on
ahead to cross the ford on the Spruit, supposedly with the
mounted infantry ahead as scouts, while the cavalry withdrew more slowly. It was not then realised that De Wet
with a strong force of Boers was in position at Sanna's
Ford on the Spruit waiting for the column to cross, but
Boer cavalry were seen on the right flank.

The mounted infantry were not in front of the wagons
as they should have been and as the column approached the
Ford they were met without warning by a withering fire.
The column's rear was now threatened by artillery, there
were Boers on the right flank and the front was strongly
held. Only the left remained open and the Tenth and
Household Cavalry were ordered to try to cross the Spruit
on that side. Meanwhile at the Ford there was a scene of
wild confusion with riderless horses and driverless wagons
and gun teams careering in all directions, but the men in
charge of the regimental ammunition wagons, with a highly
explosive load, behaved with great coolness and extricated
them from the chaos. For their bravery on this occasion
Private MacMillan and Private Tharrat received the
D.C.M.

After a considerable detour the Household Cavalry discovered a place to cross and the Tenth found one on their
left. They crossed and made for the ridge above with a
view to a flanking movement, but owing to their greatly
reduced strength were ordered to retire slowly on Spring-
fontein, where they bivouacked. The Tenth's casualties in
this ambush were three killed, five wounded, two officers
and twenty-six N.C.O.s and men missing, taken prisoner,
the two officers and several others being patients in the
ambulance wagon with enteric fever.

On April 29 the brigade marched to Krantz Kraal to
assist General Tucker in a flank movement on Welkom.
After marching and fighting actions each day with light

casualties, the battle of Welkom took place on May 4, when the regiment was in the saddle continuously from 6.45 a.m. until dark. On May 6 they occupied Winsburg without resistance and marched on to Groot Dam. On the 9th they fought at Zand River and on the 10th captured about forty prisoners and five wagons. Daily marching and continuous actions followed until they entered Pretoria in June and bivouacked six miles outside it. On June 11 at the battle of Diamond Hill, 'Q' Battery was under heavy rifle fire and was only saved by a charge of the 12th Lancers and House-hold Cavalry, with a troop of 'C' Squadron of the Tenth. Unfortunately the Earl of Airlie, by this time Colonel of the Twelfth Lancers, was killed in this action.

The regiment was then engaged in similar continuous marching and frequent actions in the Transvaal, crossing into the Orange Free State once more on June 29. On July 3 they were rejoined by eighteen men who had been captured at Sanna's Ford and imprisoned in Pretoria. The Tenth then continued in pursuit of De Wet's forces, relieving Hore's Laager, which he had beseiged, and fighting many small actions. This continued until Rustenburg was reached on September 26, 1900. In October, to the great regret of the Tenth, their old friends the Household Cavalry with whom they had fought side by side for thousands of miles, were relieved by the 8th Hussars and returned to England. At the same time Colonel Fisher-Childe's period of command came to an end and he was succeeded by Lt.-Colonel Alexander.

Based at Rustenburg until December 20 the regiment was engaged in mopping up operations, rounding up isolated parties, searching farms and destroying crops. From here the Tenth was railed to Natal Spruit and early in 1901 began their part in a big enveloping movement designed to drive the Boers towards the borders of Zululand and Swaziland. Starting with an action at Halfontein on January 12 the movement continued until April 12, but owing to heavy flooding during February and early March no supplies could reach the regiment for three weeks and, although the grazing was good, the men, already on half rations were reduced to half a pound of mealie meal per man. By the time the brigade reached Glencoe in Natal on April 12 however they had captured fifty Boers, 4,000 cattle, 15,000 sheep, 583 horses and 100 wagons.

On the day after reaching Glencoe the regiment entrained for Pretoria and another march of a similar nature followed through the Eastern Transvaal to Middleburg, which was reached on July 16. A new phase of the war then began. The brigade was split up into small columns and the 10th Hussars, with 'Q' Battery R.H.A. and a supply column, entrained for Cape Colony, where Commandant Scheepers and other Commandos were proving troublesome.

On August 4 'B' Squadron under Lord Bentinck was detached with a pom-pom section and for the next ten months acted as an independent unit in the Aberdeen, Murraysburg, Carnarvon and Colesbar areas. It performed good service, killing and capturing many Boers and protecting the lines of the blockhouses while under construction, with few casualties on their side.

H.Q., 'A' and 'C' Squadrons carried out duties of a similar kind in the Graaf Reinet area, moving towards Blavians Kloof, where they encountered superior numbers in an unassailable position and suffered some casualties. Two squadrons advancing towards Uniondale on August 19 were ambushed by overwhelming numbers near Avontuur. The order to retire to a more strategic position at the neck of the pass was given and they had to withdraw in single file over a bullet swept defile. Allowing two horse's lengths between men the dangerous area was crossed without casualties and the Boers were held back until reinforcements of the 12th Lancers arrived. Uniondale was then taken on the 21st and the pursuit of Commandant Scheepers began. It continued unceasingly until his capture on October 11 by Captain Shearman with 'A' Squadron.

Mopping up operations in difficult country involving frequent skirmishes continued until June 24, 1902, when the war finally ended. The regiment had been marching and fighting continuously for two years and seven months, operating in Cape Colony, the Orange Free State, the Transvaal and Natal. 'B' Squadron now rejoined the regiment and the Tenth was stationed for a brief period at Malmesbury where they celebrated the Coronation of King Edward VII.

On King Edward's accession to the throne on the death of Queen Victoria in 1901, Lord Ralph Kerr was appointed to the Colonelcy of the 10th Hussars, but the King himself remained as Colonel-in-Chief. When an officer of the Tenth happened to mention the deeds of his old regiment in South Africa he was gently chided:

'My old Regiment; *old* Regiment; *my* Regiment you mean!'

In 1901 another event of some significance in the regiment occurred. R.S.M. Bradshaw and S.S.M. Byart as well as some other N.C.O.s, who had returned home from South Africa, formed an Old Comrade's Association in order not to lose touch with each other, agreeing to meet annually for a reunion dinner. This was at first restricted to N.C.O.s, but was soon to grow larger and become an important feature of the regimental life.

As a result of their part in the Boer War the regiment was granted the right to add 'Relief of Kimberley' and 'South Africa 1899–1902' to their Battle Honours. Apart from the regiment's own fine record, the 12th Lancers were commanded by Lord Airlie until his death, the South African Light Horse was raised and commanded by Lt.-Colonel the Hon. J. Byng and a regiment of Colonial Cavalry by Lt.-Colonel C. McM. Kavanagh, all 10th Hussars.

During the regiment's brief stay in Malmesbury Lt.-

Colonel Alexander, whose entire command had been spent in continuous action and who had been twice wounded earlier, retired to England on leave. In his place Lt.-Colonel the Hon. J. Byng was appointed to command the regiment and in September, 1902, the 10th Hussars embarked from Capetown for India once more.

Chapter
7

O N landing at Bombay in October 1902 the regiment entrained for Mhow, where they were to be stationed for the next four years. Early in his command there Colonel Byng instituted an extremely popular, though for those days revolutionary, change. He altered the issue uniform of khaki drill and had grey flannel turn down collars and khaki ties issued in their place. This caused considerable stir and Kitchener himself came to examine the change, but fortunately he approved and again the Tenth gave the lead to the rest of the army.

Unfortunately Colonel Byng had been little more than eighteen months with the regiment when a severe fall at polo resulted in his having to return to England and in 1904 he was succeeded by Lt.-Colonel C. McM. Kavanagh. Under his energetic direction the Tenth continued to excel. During manoeuvres they even succeeded on one occasion in marching a distance of ninety miles across rough country within twenty-four hours, some of the patrols then covering 120 miles, which must be nearly an all-time record.

In 1905 they encamped at Bombay, while acting as escorts during the visit of the Prince and Princess of Wales. On their return the routine of a small station continued with every sort of sport organised competitively down to troop football and cricket, as well as competitive horsemanship, rifle shooting and other more professional skills. Even so, no doubt, the majority were glad to move to Rawalpindi in 1907.

The 9th Lancers, whom they relieved there, were badly affected by malaria and conditions were bad. Lt.-Colonel John Vaughan, who now succeeded to command, at once took vigorous action against flies and mosquitoes and soon afterwards there were no further attacks. Thereafter the health of the regiment remained unimpaired.

Amongst Colonel Vaughan's innovations was the first Regimental Gazette, produced in 1907 by that most efficient Quartermaster Major Roland Pillinger, who had enlisted with the regiment as a boy in 1879. If not the first of its kind, this quarterly magazine was certainly among the first and was soon by far the best. Apart from giving Old Comrades at home news of their activities it also provided the regiment with a topic of interest in a tropical station.

To maintain the interest of the troops Colonel Vaughan also introduced friendly 'jousts,' or mixed sporting events, with the 12th Lancers and it was fitting that such a keen sportsman should himself have won the coveted Kadir Cup for pig-sticking that same year, 1907. Under his methods of training the regiment went on to win the Inter-Regimental Polo Championships each year from 1907 to 1912, a record never beaten.

In 1909, with the assistance of Major Pillinger, he produced a small Regimental History suitable for the troops to encourage their pride in the regiment. In the same year the Old Comrades Association, which had been steadily growing in numbers, was opened to all ranks. Apart from holding an Annual Old Comrades dinner, a relief fund for deserving cases was started and employment found for those requiring jobs, this welfare aspect being turned over to a separate Regimental Association in 1912.

In 1910, on the death of King Edward VII, King George V became Colonel-in-Chief. Announcing the news Colonel Vaughan added: 'Opportunity is now taken of the occasion to assure his Majesty King George, that every Officer, N.C. Officer, and man deeply appreciates the distinction bestowed upon them and the Regiment by His Majesty's succession as the supreme Tenth Hussar.'

In the same year the Tenth introduced a new method of

forming a machine gun detachment. Under Major Watkin Williams using new equipment of their own design the regiment were able to bring a machine gun into action inside fifty seconds. On visiting the Tenth General Douglas Haig was so impressed that the equipment and drill were introduced into every cavalry regiment in India and subsequently used in the 1914 War.

Colonel Vaughan was succeeded by Lt.-Colonel R. W. Barnes in 1911 and in 1912 after winning the Inter-Regimental Polo for the sixth and last time the Tenth sailed for South Africa once more. While stationed at Potchefstrom in 1913 they were employed in quelling the disturbances following the Johannesburgh General Strike and by their good humoured efforts succeeded in avoiding bloodshed. An example of their imperturbability was contained in the rejoinder of one of the troopers to a female ringleader in the crowd who had just cursed him roundly and spat at him:

'It wasn't so much what you said I was laughing at, Mam, as your face.'

When news of the outbreak of war reached them in August 1914 the regiment was engaged in manoeuvres, which were promptly cancelled. At first it was thought the Tenth and the Royals might be engaged in S.W. Africa, but orders were received to embark for England from Capetown on August 5. After a pleasant, peaceful voyage they disembarked at Southampton on September 19. They were immediately sent to Salisbury Plain as part of the 6th Cavalry Brigade with the Royals and 3rd Dragoons, receiving only seventy-two hours leave in relays, while re-equipping and preparations for service went ahead in feverish haste. Thus when they were inspected by King George they had to march past with bare swords as their scabbards were being dulled.

On October 8 the Tenth landed at Ostend, marching to Ypres. On October 13 a patrol under Lieutenant Wilson and 2nd Lieutenant the Earl of Airlie encountered a German patrol of Uhlans and lost one man wounded and captured, one of the only two P.O.W.s the Tenth lost throughout the war. On October 19 at the village of Ledeghem a German bicyclist battalion was encountered and the machine gun troop was ordered to join the advanced patrol in an estaminet outside the village. An eyewitness account of the action that followed reads:

"The Germans could be seen in the turnips in front, however the three hundred yards to the estaminet were devoid of cover and the M.G. commander gave the order to gallop. On reaching the estaminet several of the troop horses failed to respond to the aids to halt. Their riders were faced with the choice of being carried into the German lines or throwing themselves off, which they did and the horses galloped riderless into the German lines, one old grey horse trotting about amongst the turnips and Germans snorting defiance. In the end they all returned unharmed.

Meanwhile the excitement of going into action for the first time had caused even the seasoned soldiers of twelve years' service and upwards to omit quite a number of details of elementary training, however both guns were mounted at last. During all this the senior Sergeant had nearly burst himself with expletives and excitement. At last with a hoarse cry of: 'Ere, give it to me,' he hurled Nos 1 and 2 from the nearest gun and seized the traversing handle with his left hand and pulled the crank handle smartly over with his right. The failure of the gun to respond to the pressure of the double button caused another and more terrible explosion of language. No. 1 politely referred his commander's left hand to the belt and suggested a repetition of the movements of his right. All was well, for the first time we were sending real bullets at a real enemy. The cyclist battalion was completely stopped, but the withdrawal of another brigade caused us to retire also."

The Germans had successfully advanced on Mons, but the Cavalry Divisions had covered the British army detrainment in Flanders and the 6th Cavalry Brigade now fought dismounted in the trenches, relieving the Brigade of Guards on October 21. During this first Battle of Ypres they were involved in heavy fighting until November 20. Then, with a reorganisation of the Corps, the Tenth joined the 8th Cavalry Brigade with the Royal Horse Guards and Essex Yeomanry, their divisional Commander being Major-General the Hon. J. Byng.

Colonel Barnes who had been twice wounded during the first battle of Ypres was now succeeded by Lt.-Colonel Shearman. Casualties in the Tenth were seven officers and forty-seven other ranks killed, ten officers and eighty-five other ranks wounded, but the value of cavalry as a mobile reserve had by this time been proved. It was clear that the cavalry were the best all-round trained soldiers in the British Army. They could use a bayonet and throw a bomb. They were fine shots and had their own machine guns. They could and did take their place in the line whenever and wherever the situation was critical, performing all the tasks of infantry. When in reserve they were always ready as cavalry to fight mounted, continuing to look after their horses often under great difficulties, while digging reserve trench systems, or constructing roads and railways. They could use their swords and were always ready and able to provide shock tactics or scout ahead when required and, as ever, the Tenth was to the fore in all these duties.

When fighting as infantry each cavalry regiment in a brigade provided one company, thus each Brigade became a three company battalion. At Zillebeke on February 3, 1915, when the Tenth next went into the trenches with the Essex Yeomanry, the distance between the trenches was as little as twelve to fifteen yards and they were very wet. The closeness of the trenches is illustrated by the fact that a match box was thrown over to a trench occupied by the Blues, with a note: 'We are a battalion of an Alsace Regiment; don't shoot us and we won't shoot you. Vive la France, but Germany comes first.'

The stagnation and stalemate that developed with the growth of trench warfare led to ever heavier shelling and the gradual evacuation of the civilian population in the Ypres area, but no-one then foresaw three further years in the Flanders mud, or the appalling casualties to come. On May 9 the 8th Brigade were moved forward again and the Tenth took their place in the trenches for the Second Battle of Ypres. On May 13 the Germans launched their supreme effort to break the line with very heavy shelling. Colonel

Cavalry passing through a battered town.

Shearman was killed leading a counter attack which gained its objective. Casualties were heavy, but the survivors were rallied by Lieutenants Bouch and the Earl of Airlie. The Germans were held and the 8th Cavalry Brigade was eventually relieved by the 9th Cavalry Brigade. Total casualties in the Tenth were four officers and twenty-seven other ranks killed and six officers and 101 other ranks wounded. The remainder of the 8th Cavalry Brigade were then amalgamated with the 6th Cavalry Brigade.

A special order issued by the Brigade after this action said in part: 'By driving the Germans out . . . the Brigade undoubtedly saved the situation . . . we were enabled to establish an unbroken line.'

Lt.-Colonel H. F. Wickham now succeeded to command on the death of Colonel Shearman and the Tenth returned to the trenches at Hooge with their old friends the 2nd Life Guards and Royal Horse Guards. From June to September they remained in reserve, training in cavalry work, bombing and rifle practice. In September they moved to Loos and were engaged in the Battle of Loos of 1915. The town was a shambles from shelling, and still under continuous shell and machine gun fire. Bodies of our own and German dead lay everywhere, water was unobtainable and the place stank of gas. The Tenth had the job of searching the cellars and houses for prisoners and many were taken, some still in communication with their own side by telephone.

Indicative of the close relationships in the regiment was a story told of about this period by the Earl of Airlie, then an acting Captain. He had occasion to reprimand an officer recently promoted from the ranks. He was listened to in respectful silence, then the officer asked if he might say a word.

'It's an interesting fact,' he said. 'That when I joined the regiment as a private twenty-two years ago, your father gave me my first reprimand. Now his son has given me my first reprimand as an officer, and done it very well too, if I may say so, Sir.' With which he departed chuckling audibly.

On January 3 1916 the dismounted battalion was in action against the Hohenzollern redoubt and another period of trench warfare followed for six weeks, after which they retired for a further period of training at Embry and Bethune. Then on June 24 they were recalled to take part in the great Somme Offensive of 1916, mounted, but there was never any opportunity for the use of cavalry and day after day was spent in appalling conditions for men and horses. On July 4 they retired to billets and pioneer parties from each regiment were engaged in laying cables under shellfire and similar duties.

On December 22 during a bitterly cold winter the Tenth moved to billets by the sea at Merlimont and in February 1917 to the Fressin area. Here Lt.-Colonel J. P. Hardwicke took command. In the rough country round about there were herds of wild pig. A standing squadron order was that on manoeuvres 'one eye in all ranks must always be open for pig.'

On April 9 the division moved at a moment's notice to Arras. The situation here had become fluid and patrols were soon engaged with the enemy at Orange Hill. The village of Monchy-le-Preux was captured in dashing style, but here the entire force came under heavy shellfire, which striking the hard pavements caused tremendous casualties amongst horses and men. The outskirts of the village however were stubbornly held and the machine gun detachments answered the heavy machine gun fire. A counter attack seemed likely but the cavalry remained in position although the main street of Monchy was littered with dead and dying horses and men. In one place so thickly that it was necessary to climb over them to get up the street.

By April 12 the main portion of the force had been relieved, but detachments remained behind until the infantry attack of the relieving brigade proved successful and the line was straightened once more. Writing of the sur-

vivors it was said: 'You have never seen cavalry like them—
mud encrusted figures in flat metal hats, men with three
days beards and faces covered in grime in no way suggesting
the smart Lancers, Dragoons or Hussars'.

Let a survivor picture the scene at Monchy: 'We paraded
just after daylight just below the ridge on a snow covered
bleak hillside. Bugles rang out and off we went—slowly at
first, over the hill top—on past our guns and into the valley
beyond. Things now began to hum! Shrapnel shrieked and
machine guns rattled, each taking its toll. Not a man looked
back and the pace increased; our objective a village on
the next hill crest. Some wheeled right, others left, to enter
at either end. One squadron got bogged and became an
easy target for enemy machine gunners. As we dashed up
the village street, the enemy disappeared into the nearest
hole. "Dismount for action." Three-fourths of the men
hurried away to dig themselves in desperately, while the
remainder took the horses to cover behind some walls and
buildings. Our objective was gained and all seemed well.

'But the price was yet to be paid. As we looked to our
girths and adjusted saddles an enemy aeroplane droned
overhead and the airman spied us out. His starry signal had
scarce died out when a shell smashed a hole through a wall
nearby and others crashed in the street. Horses plunged
and reared, but soon became quiet when checked and never
flinched again.

'Hell now seemed let loose, houses crumbled and fell
about our ears, and men and horses were torn asunder by
evil smelling high explosives. All had work to do, perhaps
shoot a horse to end its sufferings, or tie a bandage on a
wounded pal; even a Jerry saved a Tommy's life by tying
a tourniquet on his shattered thigh. Friend and foe became
comrades thus.

'A shell burst near me. It felt like a violent shove and
warm blood spurting from a wounded horse drenched my
face. Two horses went down and it took all my strength to

drag clear a comrade who was firmly pinned beneath them. Blood mingling with slushy snow ran down the gutters. Curiously, I thought of Tennyson's "Charge of the Light Brigade" and I felt that that famous incident was child's play to this. How long it lasted I know not, for time and eternity seemed strangely mixed.

'But darkness came at last. Some thirty or so surviving horses with their attendant horsemen sadly went away. We left a thousand horses and many comrades in that village street. I rode one horse and led another that was badly wounded. To him I said: "Charlie, if you can't gallop, leave you I must," but gallop he did, like the hero he was and back we went, past our guns over the hilltop, along a shell torn track and through a deserted city. When at last we bivouacked snow was falling heavily. I and two others crouching together sheltered beneath a blanket, the snow soon covered us like a shroud, fatigue and exposure brought fitful sleep, the end of a desperate day.'

The Tenth's casualties were two officers and twenty-five other ranks killed, seven officers and 150 other ranks wounded, five missing. Total, 189.

For some weeks afterwards in comfortable billets the time was spent in reinforcing and refitting with men and horses. During June 1917 dismounted parties from each regiment in the Brigade were engaged in duties in the line, with Lt.-Colonel W. O. Gibbs now in command of the Tenth. Raiding parties and trench digging were the chief duties at this time. Further dismounted parties were engaged in November and December of 1917 after the German counter attack following the battle of Cambrai. This involved much night patrolling, but casualties were slight.

In February 1918 redistribution of the division resulted in the 10th Hussars returning to the 6th Cavalry Brigade with the 1st Royal Dragoons and 3rd Dragoon Guards again. This involved moving to Tertry where the Tenth were most unfortunate in receiving a direct hit with a bomb on a hut filled with troops during a night air attack. Six men were killed and thirty-four injured, of whom four subsequently died of their wounds.

On March 21 the German advance began with a tremendous bombardment and by March 23 they had broken through in several places and were only finally stopped and held at Amiens. On that day, after standing by since 4 a.m., a mounted squadron under command of Major Watkin Williams of the 10th Hussars, with three mixed troops, the first of 3rd Dragoons, the second of 10th Hussars under Lt. Viscount Ednam, the third of 1st Royal Dragoons, was ordered to support the shaky mixed force of infantry near Collezy by a cavalry charge.

On approaching Collezy the squadron came under heavy machine gun fire from Golancourt but took cover behind a farm. The first troop of 3rd Dragoons were ordered to attack a copse on the right and secure that flank. This they did successfully, chasing the enemy into the wood and dismounting and shooting them at point-blank range, taking fifteen prisoners. Meanwhile the second troop of Tenth Hussars, under Viscount Ednam with Major Watkin Williams, charged in line, with the third troop of Royals 100 yards behind them. When the charge started the men were knee to knee, but owing to the machine gun fire and the fast pace they tended to open out and when the enemy were reached were more or less extended.

The distance was about six hundred yards with the last two hundred over heavy plough under persistent machine gun fire from the left flank, but the 10th Hussars charged with drawn sabres cheering loudly and the enemy surrendered freely at the sight of them. The Tenth rode straight through the enemy, the Royals following and mopping up the parties left behind. Between seventy and 100 Germans were sabred and after the melee, on the 'Rally' being sounded 107 prisoners were taken, although the number was really larger since many gave themselves up to the infantry following the charge. Six machine guns were captured and although the casualties of the squadron were seventy-three out of 150 these were mostly wounded, comparatively few being killed.

The moral effect on the infantry was tremendous. So also was the impact on the Germans. Acknowledging this later a German officer of a dismounted cavalry regiment wrote: 'The cavalry attack of the British regiment over No Man's Land near Arras was a heroic effort . . . so courageous and well carried out that we are proud to have witnessed it.'

Meanwhile the dismounted detachment was in action and heavy fighting continued until April 4 when they were relieved by the Australians. Casualties were one officer killed, seven officers wounded, including Major Watkin Williams and Viscount Ednam, and nine other ranks killed, sixty-one wounded and fifteen missing.

On April 7 Lt.-Colonel Whitmore, who subsequently wrote a history of the 10th Hussars in the 1914–18 War took over command of the regiment. At a Brigade Show held at this time the Tenth won nearly all the prizes, including 1st and 2nd for the best conditioned troop of horses, which in these conditions was a remarkable and extremely fine achievement.

The offensive at Amiens began in August 1918 and from then on the tide of the war turned at last. The follow-up continued east of Arras, over the country near Monchy-le-Preux, so well remembered. Here the 10th Hussars were attached to a Canadian force composed of the Canadian Light Horse, armoured cars and other units, being with them at the capture of the Drocourt–Queant line. They then rejoined the 6th Cavalry Brigade.

A stubborn action at Honnechy followed. The Tenth's casualties here, caused largely by bombing and shellfire were five officers wounded, seven other ranks killed and fifty-eight other ranks wounded, also one hundred and six

The Cavalry wait behind the lines during the Arran offensive, April 1917.

horses. The Tenth then reached Manancourt and while in reserve here took advantage of the plentiful game to be seen. Major Buxton organised several shooting parties for six or seven guns and a number of good afternoon's part-ridge driving were enjoyed, with bags of fifteen to twenty brace and seven to ten hares.

On November 6 orders arrived to move north in very wet conditions. The horses were up to their knees and hocks in mud and some of the saddlery had to be dug out of the mud before saddling-up for the march. News of the Armistice was still uncertain on the morning of November 11 and orders were received to press forward as quickly as possible. The Tenth sent out two troops on reconnaissance to gain touch with the rapidly retreating enemy. One of these ran into machine gun fire and did not return until 8 p.m. The other did not contact the enemy, but did not return until the following day. Meanwhile the Tenth had reached Leuze and received orders that hostilities were to cease at 11.00 a.m.

As a result of their service during the 1914–18 War the 10th Hussars were permitted to add the following to their battle honours: 'Ypres 1914–15.' 'Loos,' 'Arras 1917–18,' 'Frezenburg,' 'Somme 1918,' 'Amiens,' 'Pursuit to Mons,' 'Avre,' 'Drocourt Queant,' 'France and Flanders 1914–1918.' Their total casualties were: fifteen officers, 199 other ranks killed, forty-one officers, 528 other ranks wounded, and two other ranks P.O.W.

After various moves the regiment was stationed at Konigshaven in December as part of the Rhine Army of Occupation. This distasteful duty only lasted six months and in 1919 under Lt.-Colonel Seymour, having been abroad for nearly twenty years, they returned to Canterbury. They had hardly settled down in England however before they were abruptly posted to the West of Ireland in April 1920, where conditions were not unlike France with the Squadrons scattered in various villages. The only difference was that due to the activities of the Sinn Feiners the inhabitants were hostile.

After the Tenth had acted as escorts to King George V at the state opening of the first Parliament of Northern Ireland, the troop train carrying H.Q. and 'B' Squadrons back from Belfast to Dublin was deliberately derailed, resulting in the guard's van being wrecked. Two of the Hotchkiss gun team travelling in the van were killed. The other, Private J. Bodill, one of a family of four brothers, sons of an old Tenth Hussar, all of whom had served in the regiment was injured.

On the regiment's return to Canterbury from Ireland H.R.H. Prince Henry, Duke of Gloucester, joined the regiment, being promoted Lieutenant in July. On this occasion the regiment was to be allowed finally a reasonable tour of home duty and in 1923 Lt.-Colonel Malise Graham assumed command.

In 1924 Major-General Sir Hugh Dawnay, Viscount Downe, died after twelve years as Colonel and thirty-eight years connected with the regiment. Appointed as his successor was Field Marshall Viscount Byng of Vimy, then Governor-General of Canada, whose association with the regiment extended back to the Afghanistan War. In the same year the regiment was posted from Canterbury to

H.R.H. Prince Henry, Duke of Gloucester, as a lieutenant in the 10th Hussars at the Trooping of the Colour in 1923.

Aldershot, where they remained until they moved to Hounslow in 1927. During those years 1925, 1926 and 1927 came the series of wonderful wins in International Show Jumping events by Colonel Malise Graham and that remarkable horse 'Broncho.'

The year 1927 also saw the *Gazette* republished under the able editorship of Major C. K. Davy. In the first issue note was taken of the creeping mechanisation of the cavalry. The regiment now had on its official strength, fourteen motor lorries, three motor cycles and three motor cycle combinations, but danger of complete mechanisation still seemed distant.

Lt.-Colonel V. J. Greenwood assumed command in 1928 and as a valedictory feat the regiment won the Inter-Regimental Polo at Roehampton before departing for Cairo, where they were stationed for a further year before moving on to Meerut in 1930. It was perhaps a sign of the times that Lt. Ronald King flew back from leave to Cairo in a Gipsy Moth, before the Tenth were posted to India.

Relieving the 4th Hussars at Meerut the regiment un-expectedly found an old Tenth Hussar already there. The horse known as 'Old Timer' had first joined the Tenth in 1908. Left with the 21st Lancers in 1912 he had served in action and been wounded on the N.W. Frontier, subse-quently proving a fine show jumper and winning many prizes. On the arrival of his old regiment he appeared to recognise the regimental call, but by this time he was retired and allowed to roam at will round the barracks, being a great pet of all. He finally died two years later aged 34, still with the Tenth.

Lt.-Colonel Willoughby Norrie assumed command of the regiment in 1931 and for the next four years life in India continued in much the old familiar pattern. In 1932 the regiment moved to Lucknow. In 1933 they won the Inter-Regimental Polo Championship once again. In both 1932 and 1933 the Kadir Cup was won by officers of the regiment, making six times in all during the Tenth's various postings to India. Both in 1933 and 1934 the regiment had officers in the final unlucky not to win, including Colonel Willoughby Norrie himself.

As ever the Tenth remained to the forefront in sport, with football, cricket, boxing, swimming and running amongst the varied competitions organized. Regular concerts and entertainments were also arranged, in which, as ever, the band provided some outstanding performers. Amongst the last might be noted Bandsman Norman Wisdom, who ran seventh in the inter-regimental cross country run in 1934.

In 1935 Lt.-Colonel B. O. Hutchison assumed command. In the same year the Tenth learned with regret of the death of their Colonel, Viscount Byng of Vimy, who was succeeded by Brigadier General Viscount Hampden. Early in 1936 followed the death of King George V, their Colonel-in-Chief.

By this time the news of the Tenth's early return to England and imminent mechanisation was known. They gained a final valedictory victory in the Inter-Regimental Polo Championships before leaving India and their horses for ever. Captain David Dawnay went on to captain the British polo team in the Olympic Games. Then for the first time after an overseas tour the Tenth returned home to England without being involved in any fighting on the way or immediately on their return, despite every expectation of a halt en route in Palestine to deal with Arab unrest there. Fortunately there were to be nearly three years for them to learn their new role before being involved in another war. Instead, soon after their return to Tidworth, they learned of the appointment of H.R.H. the Duke of Gloucester as their new Colonel-in-Chief on the accession of George VI.

It was the end of another era.

Chapter
8

IN 1937 the 10th Hussars joined the Queen's Bays and
9th Lancers in the 2nd Cavalry Brigade and Lt.-Colonel
C. H. Gairdner succeeded to command on Colonel
Hutchison's promotion. At first mechanisation consisted
merely of equipping the regiment with 15 cwt. trucks while
courses were instituted and everyone got down seriously to
the task of mastering their new roles. Despite all the
cavalryman's natural adaptability it was a slow job without
proper equipment.

Skilled horsemen had to become equally skilled drivers
and mechanics, or learn the intricacies of wireless or tank
gunnery; the tank commanders had to master all these and
learn to direct the driver and gunner while map reading and
choosing ground across country at speed. Troop leaders had
to learn to control two other tanks as well as their own and
make instant strategical appreciations under fire, while
remaining alert for orders from their squadron leader. The
cavalryman's natural eye for country was a help, but the
transition was a hard one.

The Tenth proved that they had not entirely forgotten
horses by winning the Inter-Regimental Polo Championship at Hurlingham, the first time any regiment had succeeded in winning the Championship in India one year and
in England the next. Major G. M. Roddick also won the
Military Gold Cup and went on to do so for the next two
years, thus establishing another record for the Tenth.

By 1938 the regiment had acquired some obsolete
eighteen-year-old Mark IV light tanks and a number of
Bren carriers in addition to their 15 cwts and were at least
becoming accustomed to tactical manoeuvring and other-

wise operating in their new sphere. The 1938 Crisis came and went, leaving a rash of trenches and a determination to prepare for the war that was obviously coming.

Early in 1939, under the new rule then instituted, Viscount Hampden relinquished the Colonelcy on becoming seventy and Colonel V. J. Greenwood was appointed his successor. In April of the same year the Royal Armoured Corps was formed and the 10th Hussars became part of the new Corps, the 2nd Cavalry Brigade becoming the 2nd Armoured Brigade. This did not prevent the Tenth winning the Inter-Regimental Polo Championship again in June and on the turf they were well represented by Majors G. M. Roddick and C. B. Harvey amongst others.

Throughout 1939 however the picture was one of steadily increasing mobilisation and preparation for war. Even so the 1st Armoured Division, of which the 2nd Armoured Brigade was part, was not nearly fully equipped at the outbreak of war in September. The Tenth and the other regiments in the Brigade had only one squadron of the new cruiser tanks and otherwise were still equipped with the obsolete Mark IVs armed only with heavy machine guns.

Due to this and the return of reservists still largely untrained in mechanized warfare the 1st Armoured Division did not join the B.E.F., but was allotted the task of defending the east coast from the Wolds to Harwich while they continued training. The Tenth were stationed at Newmarket amongst many old friends and Thetford Heath proved a useful training ground. In January 1940 they moved to Wimborne into comfortable squadron billets near Holt, where more tanks began to arrive, so that they were soon nearly up to war establishment.

In April 1940 Lt.-Colonel Hignett assumed command and with all the false confidence of that 'Phoney War' period the 1st Armoured Division was ordered to move to a training area north-west of Le Mans on May 13. Then on May 10 the Germans invaded Holland and outflanked the

Maginot Line, on which the French had pinned their faith. The Division was at once warned to prepare for immediate action, but orders succeeded counter orders even as they left.

On May 21, the day the German Army encircled the B.E.F., the regiment embarked from Southampton. Frantic efforts had been made to complete their equipment, but, even so, many of the 2 pounder guns were still in crates lashed to the sides of the tanks. Course was set for Le Havre, but owing to the approach of the German forces was changed en route for Cherbourg where they arrived at dawn on the 22nd.

The Tenth disembarked and fitted out their tanks at once. While waiting to entrain they helped to load Rolls Royce engines from some newly arrived travel-stained R.A.F. transporters onto the ship they had just left. Although unaware of the importance of this at the time, or the reason for the R.A.F.'s haste, it may well have helped to win the Battle of Britain four months later and was probably their most constructive action towards winning the war while in France.

After entraining, they concentrated north-west of Le Mans in their proposed training area on May 23. At 3.00 a.m. the following morning orders arrived to march to Aumont, south of the Somme, where they duly arrived at 10.00 a.m. after passing a machine-gunned column of refugees by the roadside. Here they had their first experience of bombing and shelling and Lt. Richmond was killed while reconnoitring a bridge, the Tenth's first casualty of the war.

On May 25, by which time the B.E.F. was in a hopeless position, the 2nd Armoured Brigade was placed under French command, minus their artillery and infantry, who had already been diverted elsewhere. On May 27 the day the Belgians capitulated, orders were received to attack German held bridgeheads over the Somme near Huppy, with the firm promise of French infantry and artillery support.

Even had such support been forthcoming it would have been a desperate enough plan attacking a prepared position with light tanks, but as it was it proved disastrous. The Tenth attacked at the agreed time, with 'B' and 'C' Squadrons forward and 'A' in reserve, straight into the rising sun, which made observation extremely difficult. They were heavily engaged with anti-tank guns sited in slit trenches in a strong position when news finally reached them that the French were not ready and the start had been delayed an hour. By this time many of the light Mark VI tanks with which half of each squadron was equipped were already out of action and it was too late to call off the attack. The Tenth continued to fight on alone.

Imperial War Museum

Light tanks of the Tenth destroyed during the action at Huppy.

Many gallant actions were fought. 2nd Lieutenant
Milbanke had two tanks destroyed under him and was
attempting in a third to find a weak spot in the defences
when ordered to withdraw. Squadron Sergeant-Major
Canning finding his guns would not depress sufficiently to
fire into the slit trenches around him was seen to dismount
and fire his revolver at the occupants, calmly digging out a
jammed case with his pen-knife. A member of another tank
crew in similar circumstances was seen to lay about him
with the heavy crowbar off his tank.

Although the attack penetrated about six hundred yards
and was pressed home with the reserve squadron, the enemy
defences were so strong and in such depth that it was
obviously impossible to hope to overcome them or outflank
them. The remaining tanks were withdrawn to Hodeng-au-
Bosc, with only ten left out of the original thirty and those
mostly badly damaged. On the right the Bays also had to
withdraw and the German bridgeheads remained intact.

The next day the 51st Highland Division arrived in the
area and the 1st Armoured Division was placed under their
command, although the 2nd Armoured Brigade could now
only muster a composite regiment mainly of 9th Lancers
with a mixed squadron of Tenth and Bays. On May 31 the
remainder of the regiment left for Les Hogues, arriving on
June 1 and organising themselves as lorried infantry.
Meanwhile the evacuation of Dunkirk was taking place and
it seemed as if the 51st Highland Division and the 1st
Armoured Division were the only British troops left in
France.

On June 7 the 2nd Armoured Brigade was ordered to
withdraw south of the Seine and this was carried out with
some difficulty on roads crammed with refugees. Detachments from the Tenth were sent to blow bridges behind the
Brigade and carry out patrols with the French during which
some losses were incurred. The retreat then continued westwards, bypassing Le Mans. By June 15 the French were

on the point of collapse and the Tenth received orders to move to Brest immediately. They drove 250 miles through Brittany in seventeen hours being cheered in almost all the villages through which they passed.

That night was spent in a wood fifteen miles from Brest and the following day they were ordered to go to the Docks at 10 p.m. The remaining lorries and other vehicles were destroyed and on June 16 the regiment embarked on *Manxmaid*. Mines had been dropped at the entrance of the harbour but the captain of a cargo boat had taken a bearing on them as they fell and with a volunteer crew led the way out safely. The troops gave the vessel and skipper a cheer as they passed and returned to Plymouth without further event arriving at 8.30 p.m. on June 17, amongst the last troops to leave France.

During a period of little more than three weeks the regiment had lost all its tanks and four officers and seventeen other ranks killed, five officers and three other ranks wounded, three officers and thirty-two other ranks P.O.W. Yet this had been in no sense their fault. They were eager for a chance to revenge themselves.

The Tenth were now quartered near Longbridge Deverill in Wiltshire while they re-equipped. In October fully operational once more they moved to billets in Headley Down in Surrey where they saw the Battle of Britain won overhead. Here Major-General Willoughby Norrie took command of the 1st Armoured Division and the 1st Rifle Brigade became the 2nd Armoured Brigade infantry. Training and anti-invasion measures continued during the winter and early part of 1941. In June the 1st Armoured Division was chosen for service in the Middle East.

Lt.-Colonel C. B. Harvey now assumed command and in October the Tenth sailed from Greenock on *H.T. City of Paris*, halting briefly at Durban after rounding the Cape. Port Tewfik, Suez, was reached on November 27 and the

Imperial War Museum

Early days in the desert: Crusader tanks in action.

regiment gratefully disembarked. They were now equipped with some American Honey light tanks in addition to their own British Crusaders and, while the 8th Army was starting its assault to relieve Tobruk, they equipped at Aramiya, zeroed their guns and weathered their first sandstorm. On December 14 and 15 they set off after the 8th Army.

The tanks were railed to Mersa Matruh and then trekked in Brigade formation with 150 tanks round the Brigade navigator for 400 miles westwards. Christmas was spent in Cyrenaica a little way through the Bir Shferzan Gap and the Brigade awaited the arrival of the rest of the Division while Bardia and Sollum on the coast to the north were being stormed and the Italians forced to retreat. The 1st Armoured Division then continued through El Gobi and Bir Harmat to Antelat, where they relieved the 7th Armoured Division who withdrew to Cairo to refit.

In this short interval the troops had learned the unique feel of the desert and something of the ways of desert warfare. They learned how easy it was to get lost in that sandy emptiness without a compass, especially at night under the vast expanse of stars. They grew accustomed to billowing clouds of sand behind each vehicle, to the gritty feel of sand everywhere, in their clothes, their hair, their shoes and their food, as well as to the hordes of flies forever having to be brushed away from the face and eyes at each halt. They endured all this as well as the bitter cold of the nights and the glaring heat and mirages of each day, existing on a minimum of water, but becoming expert at bathing in a mess tin and brewing up tea over a petrol fire at every opportunity. In time they even came to like it in a perverse way.

The war in the desert had many similarities to war at sea. Navigation and mobility were all important and the side unable to move was inevitably outmanoeuvred and beaten. In this respect the Eighth Army suffered two major handicaps. Their petrol cans were weak ineffective containers which leaked easily. Hence in the bumpy desert conditions the supply, or B echelon, lorries inevitably wasted great quantities in leaking cans. This often resulted in their movements being restricted through lack of petrol. The other big disadvantage was that they were consistently out-gunned. The 50 mm. guns of the Germans were effective against their tanks at 1,000 yards. The 88 mm. at 1,500. Their 2-pounders were only effective at 500 yards, hence they always had to approach for 500 yards under fire to get within range. At this stage neither of these points was fully appreciated in England.

Thus when the regimental artillery was detached for harassing duties the Tenth lacked the petrol to train with the battery of the South African Field Regiment who replaced them. Then on January 21 Rommel advanced from El Agheila. The 2nd Armoured Brigade moved at dawn on the 22nd, with the 10th Hussars leading, across the area known as the Saunnu depression. No contact was made with the enemy and they leaguered for the night nearer the coast road.

The 10th Hussars B echelon, left in the Saunnu depression, were attacked during the night by a mixed force of Italians and Germans and forced to withdraw after a sharp engagement, but not before S.S.M. Dunk had captured thirty Italians and two officers. The following morning the 9th Lancers in the lead engaged an enemy force and the Brigade was ordered to withdraw with the 10th Hussars leading. 'B' Squadron in front near Saunnu encountered a force of fourteen enemy tanks and Colonel Harvey saw that these were heading directly for Brigade H.Q. and posed a threat not only to them, but to the 22nd Guards Brigade on the coast road, as well as our harassing forces stuck in deep sand there. He therefore engaged 'A' and 'C' Squadrons as well as 'B' to draw the enemy off and a running fight ensued. Under cover of our own and artillery smoke the Tenth pressed home the attack to 500 yards and knocked out seven of the enemy, damaging others severely, but themselves lost twenty-seven tanks in all with five officers and twelve other ranks killed, twenty other ranks wounded and eight P.O.W.

The wounded and knocked out tank crews rallied under Major Wingfield and most of them managed to join 'B' echelon the following morning. Meanwhile the remains of the Tenth under Colonel Harvey, reduced to a composite squadron of seven tanks, was engaged with another force of tanks, finally rejoining the Brigade on the following morning and acting as rearguard for their retreat. A mixed enemy column of light tanks and anti-tank guns tried to cut them off from the Brigade, but Colonel Harvey charged its centre and with some losses on both sides succeeded in breaking through them. Despite the regiment's heavy losses it had been successful in saving Brigade H.Q. and the Brigade of Guards from attack by a strong armoured at a critical time.

The 2nd Armoured Brigade withdrew to Charuba, where the Tenth retired to the rear area to refit. Here 'C' Squadron was equipped with General Grant tanks and as these carried a 75 mm. gun this raised morale considerably. Their defect was that the gun was in the hull, not the turret, and the tank had to be very exposed to fire it. All the same it was an improvement on the 2-pounder.

Rommel again attacked on May 26 and the battle of Knightsbridge began. The plan was to trap Rommel's forces in a series of heavily defended box formations, cutting off his supplies. On the morning of May 27 the Brigade, 10th Hussars leading, went into action against a screen of approaching 88 mm. anti-tank guns, successfully driving them back without loss to themselves by skilful use of the ground.

At dawn on May 28 the Brigade headed north with the Tenth still leading. Contact was made with a force of anti-tank guns and 'C' Squadron engaged, but having to expose so much of their tanks in order to fire suffered some casualties. 'B' Squadron then attacked in two waves with artillery support from the H.A.C., successfully overrunning the enemy, capturing thirty-five prisoners and destroying six guns with few casualties.

The next attack was launched on a two regimental front with the 10th Hussars on the left and 9th Lancers on the right. The setting sun blinded drivers and commanders and 'A' Squadron went too wide and too deep into the midst of the enemy anti-tank guns. These were forced to withdraw, but not before inflicting casualties on the squadron and capturing most of them, including the squadron leader, Major R. A. Archer Shee.

On the next day, the 29th, at 7.30 a.m. the Tenth were engaged in a fierce battle with a force of 160 tanks. The regiment stood its ground throughout the day, but all 'B' Squadron tanks were destroyed and by 6.00 p.m. they had fought until they had no shells left to fire or tanks fit to fight. Meanwhile at Rommel's H.Q. for thirty-six hours Major R. A. Archer Shee was standing by with a white flag and proposals for a truce to hand. With his supply route cut Rommel was within hours of defeat.

On May 30 the Tenth managed to provide eight battle-worthy tanks to join the Brigade for further action, while the regiment withdrew to Sollum for a refit. Then the enemy finally succeeded in breaking through to their hard-pressed forces and very shortly afterwards the defensive boxes were overrun or forced to retreat. Tobruk fell and the rest of the Eighth Army was soon retreating helter-skelter back to the Alamein Line.

Lt.-Colonel J. P. Archer Shee now assumed command and a composite regiment of 10th Hussars, 9th Lancers and Bays was engaged at the battle of Alam Halfa with the 7th Armoured Division. On the 10th of September, after Rommel's final bid to break through at Alamein had failed, they rejoined the 1st Armoured Division. The regiment was then equipped with Sherman tanks and twelve scout cars for reconnaissance.

With the new 75 mm. gun on the Sherman tank it was possible to develop a technique of indirect fire. Major Henri Le Grand, a Belgian officer attached to the regiment at this time, had been a 75 mm. artillery officer and was of great assistance in demonstrating this method. Thus units of the 2nd Armoured Brigade and the 10th Hussars in particular were the first to adopt this style of firing, which was subsequently adopted and taught throughout the army.

The Battle of Alamein began on October 23 after considerable preparation, tanks in the assembly areas being camouflaged with sun shields to resemble lorries. The divisional plan was to attack down the coast road after a breakthrough, with the final objective known as Kidney Ridge. The 10th Hussars were on the left behind the 51st Highland Division and a tremendous bombardment was put down. The advance was slow and the Highlanders were held up, so that at dawn the regiment was ordered to deploy between mine fields. During the day the new gunnery methods proved their worth and 88 mm. guns ranging on the tanks were destroyed at long range.

The regiment moved up to support the Gordons on Kidney Ridge and in the process several tanks were knocked out, but in return several enemy tanks were also knocked out by indirect fire. The nights were spent in leaguer protected by lorried infantry and by day the tanks were replenished with ammunition two or three times, the 'B' echelon drivers coming up very courageously into the battle area to keep them supplied. Repairs were also carried out under fire. On the 29th the regiment was withdrawn, having only lost six tanks destroyed, the others that had been damaged being recoverable. On the credit side they claimed twenty-seven German and four Italian tanks burnt out, fifteen German and four Italian knocked out, but not burnt, two 88 mm., two 76 mm., ten other anti-tank guns, three

self-propelled guns and nine lorries all knocked out and
counted on the ground.

At 2.00 a.m. on the morning of November 2 the regiment
advanced on the left of the Brigade, knocking out four tanks
beyond a gap in a minefield and advancing towards Tel-el-
Aqqaqir. An enemy tank counter attack was heavily defeated and the feature was captured that night by the 1st
K.R.R.C. At dawn the Tenth came to their support to repel
a tank counter attack. Though under heavy fire all day
there were few casualties.

On November 4 the Brigade, with the 10th Hussars

Imperial War Museum

Captain Grant-Singer, who captured General von Thoma.

leading made a further advance of 4,000 yards before encountering tanks and anti-tank guns. Six were knocked out
and Captain G. A. Singer in the reconnaissance troop captured General Von Thoma, commanding the German
forces in Rommel's absence. Thus, as when General
Desnouettes was captured by Private Grisdall at the battle
of Benevente, the enemy may well have been disorganised
at a critical period.

Lt.-Colonel J. P. Archer Shee was now forced to retire
with a poisoned arm the result of a wound received on
October 24 and Major Wingfield took command, subse-

Imperial War Museum
On the road to Gabes.

quently being appointed Lt.-Colonel. The advance continued through the night and the next day, but by November 6 at 8.00 p.m. petrol supplies were exhausted and owing to the difficult going the 'B' echelon were delayed for two days. The coast road was then finally cut at Charing Cross. The 7th Armoured Division next took up the pursuit and on November 15 the 1st Armoured Division handed over its tanks to them. Meanwhile news of the North African landings had arrived and morale was high.

The 2nd Armoured Brigade was then in reserve for several months engaged in back area duties and reorganisation and refitting until preparations were made to break the Mareth Line in March 1943. On March 20 the regiment as part of the Brigade was engaged in support of the 51st Highland Division near the coast. On March 23 the 1st Armoured Division was switched southwards in a bold encircling movement to join the New Zealanders under General Freyberg in the south and break through there. The regiment was moved on transporters through the night joining the New Zealanders in the early hours of March 24.

The attack was planned with the 9th Lancers on the left and Bays on the right with the 10th Hussars covering the soft skinned Brigade echelon as rearguard. The plan was to move right through the New Zealanders regardless of how their attack had gone and continue the advance after the moon had risen. The New Zealanders attacked at 6.00 p.m. and at 8.00 p.m. the 2nd Armoured Brigade moved through them, fortunately concealed by a providential dust storm. About 10.00 p.m. the column halted fifteen miles short of El Hamma, their objective.

By this time a good many prisoners had been taken and they were joined by the Corps Commander, Lt.-General Brian Horrocks. At around midnight the moon rose and the advance continued, spreading confusion behind the enemy lines. Flaming vehicles were to be seen on all sides and an idea of the chaos caused may be gained from the fact that a battery of 88 mm. guns surrendered to the Padre of the 9th Lancers, who had mistaken them for his 'B' echelon.

El Hamma was reached at dawn and the Tenth staged a diversionary attack while the New Zealanders and 8th Armoured Brigade bypassed it. The regiment remained screening El Hamma while the rest of the division followed the New Zealanders, but on March 29 the enemy withdrew and the advance continued.

Actions followed at the pass in Djebel Fatnassa and Metzzouna, while desert gave way to scrubby plain and American voices could increasingly be heard on the wireless sets. Finally the Brigade halted at Bou Thadi on April 10. Then on the 13th the 1st Armoured Division was transferred to the 1st Army for the final battle in Tunisia.

The tanks were hastily painted green instead of desert yellow and on the night of April 14, the Brigade moved at night through the Faid Pass, Sheitla and Sheiba to Le Kef, arriving in daylight in surprisingly European surroundings. There the regiment was recognized by an N.C.O. in the R.A.O.C., who shouted out:

''Ere comes the Shiny Tenth!'

There was little of the Shiny Tenth apparent in the tanks laden with bedding rolls on the back and blackened brew cans and occasional chickens hanging behind, nor in the officers in desert boots and corduroy trousers whitened by dust and sun, with coloured scarves tucked into their bush shirts, but the spirit that had triumphed in the Boer War and the 1914 War and as far back as Waterloo and Warburg remained the same.

On April 20 the Brigade moved forward to the assembly area at Bou Arada and on the morning of the 21st advanced up the Gibellat valley through corn six feet high with strong points in scattered farm houses. The next day they counter-marched to relieve the 26th Armoured Brigade and the 10th Hussars took over from the 17th/21st Lancers. Ordered to advance they destroyed eleven enemy tanks and

Imperial War Museum

In the later stages of the Tunisian Campaign.

two anti-tank guns in a short space of time, drawing back as darkness fell. Then after enduring a day's shelling they were relieved by the Bays. On May 2 they relieved the 9th Lancers and on the 3rd carried out an indirect armour-piercing fire with a group of tanks on a force of enemy tanks, probably the first time this had ever been attempted.

On May 7 the final advance began with the 10th Hussars leading and 250 stragglers from the Herman Goering Division were captured. On May 9 'C' Squadron was left to act as flank guard to the lines of communication and knocked out three tanks, accepting the surrender of others. The enemy were now trapped and thousands of prisoners began to appear. By the 12th it was all over and on the 13th the campaign officially ended.

The regiment concentrated at Grombalia and so many captured vehicles had been added to the strength that when they were abruptly ordered to Soliman they could barely find enough drivers for this 'ghost' column. When ordered to hand these all over to the First Army on their return to the Eighth Army at Tripoli it was found difficult to comply as many of their own vehicles had been to Saunnu and back in 1942 and now were past work. Eventually matters were sorted out and they moved to Azzizia twenty miles south of Tripoli. On June 21 they were inspected there by H.M. King George VI.

On June 23 they moved to the sea fifteen miles west of Tripoli and many of the tanks were handed over to the 7th Armoured Division as the 1st Armoured Division was to be held in reserve for several months. News then arrived that they were moving to Algiers and soon afterwards Lt.-Colonel D. R. B. Kaye assumed command of the regiment. The move began in August and after a short period guarding vast numbers of P.O.W.s at Medjes-el-Bab they reached Boufarik, near Algiers, on September 30. There they were stationed in squadron billets in wine stores, which proved very comfortable.

Reinforcements arrived and the period was spent in exercises and training, particularly in indirect fire, which was later found very effective in Italy. Meanwhile the invasion of Sicily and the mainland progressed successfully and finally the 1st Armoured Division moved to Italy in May, 1944, the Tenth arriving at Naples on the 27th, after two days at sea. A few days later they moved across Italy to some twenty-five miles south of Bari, where their tanks, which had come by a different route, joined them.

Towards the end of June the Tenth was detached from the Brigade and sent just south of Rome. A period of training in close co-operation with infantry ensued and the regiment was again inspected by H.M. King George VI. While in the vicinity of Rome a 'Shiner's Club' was established in the city, but orders to rejoin the 2nd Armoured Brigade arrived before the end of July. Early in August the Tenth finally rejoined the Brigade at Ortona on the Adriatic coast for the impending attack on the Gothic Line.

On August 17 the regiment was assembled near Ancona. The attack on the Gothic Line began on August 25 and on September 2 the 1st Armoured Division joined V Corps ready for the advance, which it was optimistically hoped would not stop short of Vienna. The plan was that once the Gothic Line was broken the 1st Armoured Division would exploit the break-through. This even extended to the provision of artificial moonlight by searchlights en route, but it overlooked the fact that the tanks had mostly already exceeded their track mileage by several thousand miles and were in no state for such a venture. At that stage all new war equipment was being diverted to the 2nd Front.

On the night of September 2–3 the regiment had moved up to the south bank of the Foglia after a long and tiring march. By midnight on the 3rd they were on their way again with the 1st K.R.R.C. leading the division. The march was even more difficult than the previous day's with clouds of choking white dust, precipitous tracks and hairpin

Imperial War Museum

Sherman tanks during the assault on the Gothic Line.

bends, through cleared minefields and other defences of the Gothic Line.

At 8.00 a.m. on the 4th the Tenth reached the river Conca. Here vehicles of Divisional H.Q. were found blocking the crossing, brewing up and playing a gramophone, unaware that a battle was about to take place nearby. They were suitably dispersed by Colonel Kaye, but a mile further on tanks and troops, soon identified as Canadians, were seen in action ahead.

It was obvious at once, even had the tanks been fit for it, that there was to be no easy exploitation through to Vienna. The Tenth spent the rest of the morning observing the battle and being shelled spasmodically. Then, at 1.30 p.m. came the orders to attack. Preparations were minimal, reconnaissance restricted and information scanty and inaccurate. Not even the start line was secure and there was no infantry support. The result, as might have been anticipated, was not a success. The two forward squadrons, 'A' and 'C,' soon came under heavy shellfire and several casualties were incurred. The Colonel's tank also received a direct hit from a mortar shell, the adjutant Captain Viscount Ednam and the second-in-command Major M. F. Morley being wounded. Other casualties soon followed and the regiment was forced to withdraw behind an infantry screen at San Clemente.

While in reserve the following day further unfortunate casualties resulted from accurate shelling. On September 7, however, a dawn attack on the San Sevino ridge was successful in capturing some fifteen Germans and killing some thirty more. The squadrons were in action here in support of the lorried infantry for several days, alternating in turn, the others standing by in reserve in case of a counterattack.

On September 12 the regiment ranged on targets for a fire support task preparatory to the Ghurkas attacking the San Sevino–Passano ridge, firing as many as 840 rounds.

The attack was thoroughly successful and 1,000 prisoners were taken. The regiment then moved on to the Ripa Bianca ridge on September 15, preparatory to supporting the Ghurkas in crossing the river Marano.

On September 17 'B' Squadron crossed the river to support the Ghurkas and endured a day of heavy shelling. The Ghurkas continued to move forward slowly with the regiment in support. On the night of September 22 they crossed the river Marrechia, using their Kukries freely, leaving slit trenches full of headless corpses, but they were soon pinned down by heavy shellfire and when the regiment arrived at the river at dawn they found no crossing marked. Despite this 'A' and 'C' Squadrons crossed successfully and held the position while the Ghurkas withdrew.

In these operations in September the Tenth lost three officers and four other ranks killed and eleven officers and twelve other ranks wounded. The 2nd Armoured Brigade was then detached from the 1st Armoured Division and came under command of the 46th Infantry Division. The 1st Armoured Division was subsequently disbanded. A fresh phase had begun.

The Eighth Army had now entered the Po Valley, but with the start of heavy rain the going became extremely bad. The regiment next moved up on October 18 to the support of the 139th Infantry Brigade, aiding the 16th D.L.I. in the capture of Cesena. This was their first experience of street fighting and also their first encounter with the Partisans, who welcomed them enthusiastically. By October 20 the town was finally cleared of enemy. On the 22nd the regiment rejoined the 2nd Armoured Brigade and retired to rest at Camerano.

On November 12 the regiment moved forward again and active patrolling followed in very soggy conditions with a view to crossing the Cosina Canal. This proved difficult due to the sodden state of the ground, but close co-operation with infantry and calling down air attacks by wireless for the first time was tried out effectively. On November 18 an attack at Castiglione with air support and indirect fire proved a success. A Brigade attack on the Cosina Canal followed on November 19 with the aid of bridging tanks, which also proved successful.

The next objective was the crossing of the river Marzeno, which was achieved on November 24 by troops of 'C' Squadron and infantry. Another attack on a prominent piece of ground commanding the advance followed on the 25th and again success was achieved in co-operation with infantry. On the 3rd and 4th the Tenth gave supporting fire during the crossing of the Lamone river and then retired for a well-earned rest.

On December 14 the regiment came under the command of the 56th Infantry Division on the left flank of V Corps. This period did not last long and consisted chiefly of acting as supporting artillery, but ranging by air observation proved effective and was used in the capture of Faenza by the 2nd New Zealand Division. Tank movement was severely restricted due to mines and demolitions, but co-operation with the infantry continued with squadrons engaged singly in small local operations.

A more offensive operation took place on January 4 in conjunction with the 2nd R.T.R. and the Canadian 2nd Infantry Brigade. This involved the use of 'cab rank' aircraft called down to attack accurately only just ahead of the leading tanks. The use of tracked 'Kangaroos' to bring up the infantry quickly and the frozen state of the ground greatly aided matters. The salient which had been causing trouble was thus completely eliminated.

On January 16 the Tenth withdrew to rejoin the 2nd Armoured Brigade and were then given little more than a week to organize themselves as infantry into three dis-mounted squadrons and a machine-gun troop, the recon-naissance troop, armed with ·5-inch Brownings. The tanks were left behind and on February 1 the regiment left for

Imperial War Museum

105 mm. Sherman tanks giving infantry support towards the end of the war in Italy.

the front line to allow the exhausted infantry a chance to recuperate. The whole area had become so waterlogged that dug-outs were useless and fighting had been nearly brought to a standstill, but patrolling took place by day and night, some prisoners being taken and some casualties suffered. The ground floors of houses strengthened with timber and sand bags were the only shelter available to either side and were constantly shelled.

The Tenth were relieved on March 2 by the 1st Argyll and Sutherland Highlanders. On March 14 training began again with the 56th Infantry Division for an armoured

Imperial War Museum

Outside a molasses factory: a tank of the 10th Hussars bogged in a treacle-filled bomb crater during the advance to Ferrara.

advance with the infantry in Kangaroos. Between April 1 and 3 the regiment moved to an assembly point about five miles north-west of Ravenna. As a subsidiary to the main Divisional attack a water borne attack supporting Commandos and the 24th Guards Brigade followed on April 5-6. Enemy strong points proved troublesome, but armour piercing shells were effective on them and despite casualties the regiment continued to advance on pontoons across the flood waters.

This diversionary attack was successful and on April 10 the main Divisional attack began with a heavy air offensive. On April 11 the regiment advanced with squadrons attached to infantry brigades. Further combined squadron and infantry brigade operations continued throughout April, with inevitable casualties in some bitter fighting, 'A' Squadron supporting the Guards Brigade and 'B' and 'C' with the 169 and 167 Infantry Brigades respectively. Lt. W. G. Waugh and Sergeant W. Fairhill, D.C.M., both desert veterans, were killed amongst others at this late stage. This last action in Italy was fought on April 27 although the cease fire did not officially follow for another week. The final end of hostilities in Italy came with Field Marshall Kesselring's surrender on May 2.

The Regimental Battle Honours were: 'Saunnu,' 'El Alamein,' 'El Hamma,' 'Gazala,' 'Tunis,' 'Santarcangelo,' 'Coriano,' 'Valli di Commachio,' 'Argenta Gap.' The Tenth's total casualties during the war were: killed, twenty-nine officers, 130 other ranks, wounded, forty-four officers, 178 other ranks, P.O.W., sixteen officers, of whom several escaped, seventy-seven other ranks.

In May the regiment moved to Trieste and at the end of the year they left the 2nd Armoured Brigade, in which they had fought throughout the war, to become the divisional armour of the 46th Infantry Division in Austria. Another move quickly followed to the 49th Infantry Division near Menden, and from there to Lubeck on the Baltic.

In 1946 Lt.-Colonel J. P. Archer Shee, M.C., resumed command of the regiment and in the autumn the *Regimental Gazette* was restarted again. In the same year Lt.-General Sir Willoughby Norrie succeeded Colonel V. J. Greenwood as Colonel. Although the regiment suffered from frequent changes of division its roles remained the same and with the onset of the 'Cold War' a constant stream of National Servicemen passed through the ranks for training. Despite this, the old keenness on sport and horses continued to manifest itself, in the regimental pack of hounds, in racing and show jumping and many other ways, throughout all the changes of 1947 and 1948, including a move to Iserlohn.

In 1948 Lt.-Colonel A. Abel Smith succeeded to the command of the regiment and in 1949 Lt.-General Sir Charles Gairdner followed Lt.-General Sir Willoughby Norrie as Colonel. A change of role from divisional reconnaissance to divisional anti-tank regiment followed in 1950 and training of National Servicemen amidst Nato exercises continued throughout this period in Iserlohn, but in spite of everything the regimental spirit and keenness on sport remain unchanged. The same friendliness and keenness also appeared to animate the affiliated regiments, the Royal Wiltshire Yeomanry and the 10th Australian Light Horse.

Lt.-Colonel M. F. Morley succeeded to command in 1951 and in 1952 Brigadier C. B. Harvey was appointed Colonel. It was thus appropriate that in 1952 and 1953 the regiment won the Rhine Army Show Jumping Championships and the Army Hunter Trials. Then in 1953 the Tenth returned home for the first time in fourteen years and two peaceful if busy years at Tidworth followed with the regimental role changed yet again to armoured regiment equipped with Centurion tanks. In 1955 Lt.-Colonel A. Tuck succeeded to command of the regiment and eighteen months in Aqaba in Jordan followed, with the Tenth playing a difficult peace keeping role throughout the Suez crisis.

Returning home to Tidworth in 1957 they succeeded in winning the Captains and Subalterns' Polo Championship before returning to Munster in 1958. Here Lt.-Colonel J. Ward Harrison took command and the regiment reverted to its previous role of supporting infantry brigades by squadrons affiliated to them. This was followed by a move to Paderborn in 1960, where they changed role yet again, joining an armoured Brigade with the Greys and 3rd R.T.R. The Military Gold Cup was won in the same year by Captain P. Bengough, carrying on an old tradition. The regiment also won the B.A.O.R. Pentathlon amongst other sporting achievements.

1961 was the bi-centenary of the Battle of Warburg, included in the regimental battle honours at which time the regiment was also stationed in Paderborn. It was thus fitting that the Guidon Parade, with march off of the last Drum Horse and drum banners, and presentation of a new Guidon by the Colonel-in-Chief, H.R.H. the Duke of Gloucester, should take place here. It was an occasion of great ceremony and solemnity and a magnificent parade by the regiment in their finest traditions.

The Tenth also won the Captains and Subalterns' Polo again that year as well as the following year, 1962, when Major-General Sir David Dawnay was appointed Colonel and Lt.-Colonel W. S. P. Lithgow assumed command. By this time National Service had ended and the regiment was now at last entirely composed of regulars again. The tremendous impact of this was seen in 1963 with the regiment competing and winning in almost every sport from judo and skiing, to rowing, running, fencing and boxing, crowning it all by winning the Army F.A. Cup.

In 1964 they returned briefly to Tidworth converting their role yet again to armoured cars and moving to Aden, being posted in squadrons in Radfan, the Muscat and Oman, and Yemen Borders, being sniped and shot at throughout this period of active service. They returned to

Imperial War Museum

Guidon presentation parade, 1961.

Munster by air with Lt.-Colonel Willis in command in 1965.

In 1968 the regiment once again won the Inter-Regimental Polo Championship (B.A.O.R.) continuing their role of armoured car and air reconnaissance, by this time with their own helicopter troop. So many and so frequent had these changes been since the war that the old regimental interpretation of the motto 'Ich Dien,' 'I serve,' as 'I'll do it, what is it?' might well have applied. Yet throughout this period the regimental spirit remained unchanged and unshaken.

Since 1899 the regiment had spent barely fourteen and a half years at home. They had seen a bewildering number of changes, yet they continued to set the highest standards in work and sport. It was perhaps typical that Lt.-Colonel J. B. Willis, son of a keen Tenth Hussar, R.Q.M.S. W. N. Willis, should be succeeded in 1968 by Lt.-Colonel B. C. Greenwood, grandson and son of a Tenth Hussar, whose father had been in command of the regiment and also Colonel.

With the son and grandson of Colonels-in-Chief as Colonel-in-Chief and the grandson of a Colonel of the regiment as Colonel of the regiment, it is no surprise to learn that the adjutant's father was also once Colonel of the regiment, nor that eight officers, one warrant officer, one sergeant and several other ranks were sons of Tenth Hussars. Some of the names in the regiment indeed could be found on the rolls as far back as the eighteenth century. No wonder there was a spirit of continuity which remained unshaken by change.

In October 1969 the 10th Royal Hussars (Prince of Wales's Own), 'The Shiners,' merged with the 11th Hussars (Prince Albert's Own), 'The Cherrypickers,' to form the Royal Hussars (Prince of Wales's Own). Their cap badge contains the three royal plumes and the words 'Royal Hussars.' Their motto is 'Ich Dien,' once proudly worn by the Tenth, and they wear the distinctive cherry coloured trousers of the Eleventh. A great tradition has not ended. It goes on; Shiners and Cherrypickers together, outshone by none.

'Once a Royal Hussar, always a Royal Hussar.'

REGIMENTAL MARCH PAST

10th ROYAL HUSSARS (P.W.O.)

"The Merry Month of May"

1st B♭ CORNET

Published by Authority
Arr. by M. ROBERTS

BIBLIOGRAPHY

Historical Record of The Tenth, the Prince of Wales's Own Royal Regiment of Hussars, by Richard Cannon. 1843.

The Memoirs of the Tenth Royal Hussars (Prince of Wales's Own), by Colonel R. S. Liddell. 1891.

A Short History of the Xth (P.W.O.) Royal Hussars, by Lt.-Colonel John Vaughan and Major Pillinger. 1909.

The 10th (P.W.O.) Royal Hussars and Essex Yeomanry During the European War 1914–1918, by Lt.-Colonel F. H. D. C. Whitmore, C.M.G., D.S.O., etc. 1920.

History of the 6th Cavalry Brigade 1914–1918, by Lt. J. B. Bickersteth, M.C., 1st Royal Dragoons. 1920.

The Reminiscences and Recollections of Captain Gronow: 1810–1860. Four Volumes: 1862–1866.

To Mr. Davenport. Letters of Major Richard Davenport: Published for the Society for Army Historical Research; Special Publication No. 9. Gale and Polden, 1968.

The Trial of Colonel Quentin. 1814.

Duelling Days in the Army, by William Douglas. 1887.

Soldiering in Sunshine and Storm, by William Douglas. 1887.

An Encyclopedia of Rural Sports, by D. Blaine. 1840.

Reminiscences by Colonel Robert Spottiswoode: 1841–1935.

The 10th Royal Hussars in the Second World War 1939–1945. Edited by Committee. 1948.

Diaries: Sir John Slade; Captain Gordon; Colonel C. C. Molyneux, etc.